The **CORE**
Explained
MSLs

GW00492972

Steve Gray

ISBN 978-1-78963-030-5

Published by
The Choir Press, Gloucester in conjunction with
Compliance Hub

contents

section 4
customer service

Introduction

Welcome to the second edition of *The Code Explained for MSLs*. The intention behind this book is to help the reader understand the principles and practical implications of the Association of the British Pharmaceutical Industry's (ABPI) Code of Practice.

The book is suitable for anyone who works in a field-based scientific role for a pharmaceutical company – and all those in head office who work with them. There are also companion publications that readers may find helpful. *The Code Explained* was written specifically for head office-based employees and for those who want to know more about the wider application of the Code as it applies to other aspects of the marketing mix. The Code Explained for Pharma Reps covers those aspects of the Code relevant to sales representatives.

This edition of *The Code Explained* incorporates all the changes to the Code that became operational on 1 January 2019.

The ABPI Code covers a wide range of activities – some promotional, some strictly non-promotional. For some projects, the details of the core compliance considerations are similar – it is the intention or implementation that determines how an activity is perceived (and judged). Therefore, a key challenge for many companies is to structure and brief activities in a manner that protects the integrity of the project and thereby the integrity of the company. This book is designed to help the industry achieve, and maintain, project integrity with a particular focus on field-based scientific activities.

Thank you for your interest in *The Code Explained for MSLs*. I hope you find it useful and I am always grateful for any feedback.

Steve Gray

Steve Gray

Steven Gray is a specialist in compliance with pharmaceutical marketing codes and regulations. He has worked in the industry for over 25 years in a wide range of disciplines, from sales and marketing to medical information and compliance.

Steven holds Masters degrees in International Business Law (ILLM) and Marketing Management (MA) and is both a Chartered Marketer and a Chartered Quality Professional.

Steven has a strong reputation as an impactful, pragmatic consultant who can engage audiences at all levels within an organisation. In 2010, he launched Compliance Hub Limited, an agency that specialises in marketing and regulatory compliance within the pharmaceutical and healthcare industries. Steven is proud to name some of the pharmaceutical industry's largest and smallest businesses amongst Compliance Hub's regular client list, in addition to providing information and training resources to a large percentage of the market. You can read more about Compliance Hub in Appendix 1.

section 1
introduction and standards

chapter 1

introduction to the Code

The Code of Practice of the Association of the British Pharmaceutical Industry (ABPI) was first introduced over sixty years ago in 1958 to enhance the reputation of the industry in the eyes of the medical profession by establishing a set of standards that defined acceptable (and unacceptable) industry behaviours and practices. For a Code to be meaningful there has to be a mechanism for ensuring compliance and investigating potential breaches. This led to the establishment of the Prescription Medicines Code of Practice Authority (PMCPA), which operates independently of the ABPI and is tasked with monitoring and administering the Code and its standards.

The Code is updated on regular basis, with the most recent edition being approved by the ABPI Board of Management in 2018 and coming into effect from 1st January 2019. The actual Code contains 29 main clauses, around 200 sub- causes and numerous accompanying notes ("supplementary information"), in addition to defining the constitution of the PMCPA and the process by which complaints are investigated and adjudicated. However, the PMCPA also issues Guidance documents on specific topics; and from 2019 will also issue a Question & Answer (Q&A) list.

The use of Guidance Documents has been a feature for several years. The official position is that this "informs" regarding the interpretation of Code and have already been referenced by the PMCPA in deciding the outcome of Code cases (e.g. in a recent case against Shire regarding MSL bonuses (2987/10/17). However, experience to date is that updates to the Guidance documents are simply added to the PMCPA website without notification. They are also undated with no identifying version control, so that updates only become apparent through routine checking of the website.

The ABPI Code is written as a set of formal clauses that establish key principles by which the industry should operate. These clauses are accompanied by comprehensive 'Supplementary Information', which explains the relevant clause in more detail and also provides some examples of how the Code relates to certain activities and materials. However, the Code itself is just a framework and cannot possibly encompass every possible situation, given the innovative concepts for materials and activities that companies and agencies generate. Nor can the Code possibly keep pace with the rapid development of technological advances. The potential for uncertainty will always exist in those areas where the Code does not address the detail of the specific subject under consideration at any particular point in time. Therefore, understanding the underlying principles which should be applied becomes of fundamental importance.

This is particularly true for MSLs, who provide scientific support for HCPs but must do so in a manner that does not cross the boundaries of the Code and thereby become promotion of the unlicensed use of a medicine.

The aim of this book is to explore those underlying principles and to place them into a practical context – with the aspiration of helping the reader reach informed decisions about whether and how to proceed with planned activities.

As part of its enforcement approach the PMCPA follows best practice by publishing the outcomes of complaints, which form a bank of case precedents. These case precedents adds to our collective knowledge of the Code's interpretation without it being necessarily incorporated into the Code itself. Whilst every case is, by definition, individual and the PMCPA goes to great lengths to remind us that each case must be assessed on its own merits, the published cases nonetheless allow us to draw some strong conclusions about the correct way to apply the Code in similar circumstances. *The Code Explained for MSLs* leans heavily on case precedents, to help build the reader's understanding of the practical application of the Code. Relevant cases therefore appear regularly throughout the text.

The 13 Principles of self regulation (first articulated in the 2019 ABPI Code)

1. The pharmaceutical industry in the United Kingdom is committed to benefiting patients by operating in a professional, ethical and transparent manner to ensure the appropriate use of medicines and support the provision of high quality healthcare.
2. Patient safety is the priority. All information relating to safety must be shared accurately and transparently.
3. The aim of the Code is to ensure that the promotion of medicines to health professionals and other relevant decision makers and other activities are carried out within a robust framework to support high quality patient care.
4. Prescription only medicines must not be promoted to the public.
5. Working with patients and patient organisations can bring significant public health benefits.
6. Information about prescription only medicines made available to the public must be factual, balanced, not misleading and must not encourage prescription of a specific prescription only medicine.
7. Whilst the industry has a legitimate right to promote medicines to health professionals, the Code recognises and seeks to balance the needs of patients, health professionals and the public, bearing in mind the environment within which the industry operates and the statutory controls governing medicines.
8. The Code supports the prescribing decisions of health professionals
9. Transparency is an important means of building and maintaining confidence in the pharmaceutical industry.
10. Companies must ensure that their materials are appropriate, factual, fair, balanced, up-to-date, not misleading and capable of substantiation and that all other activities are appropriate and reasonable. Promotion must be within the terms of the marketing authorization and not be disguised. Material must be tailored to the audience.
11. Companies are responsible under the Code for the activities of their staff and third parties. Training must be provided.
12. It is a condition of membership of the ABPI to abide by the Code in both the spirit and the letter. In addition many non member companies agree to comply with the Code and accept the jurisdiction of the PMCPA.
13. Any complaint made against a company under the Code is regarded as a serious matter both by that company and by the industry as a whole. Sanctions are applied against a company ruled in breach of the Code.

chapter 2

scope of the Code

The scope of the Code includes the promotion of prescription medicines and the activities of sales representatives. However, the Code also regulates the wider nature of interactions between the pharmaceutical industry (Pharma) and its key stakeholders, such as healthcare professionals (HCPs), patients and the public. The Code therefore encompasses a wide range of non-promotional activities – primarily to ensure that these are conducted in the "right way". Typically, this means ensuring that activities truly are non-promotional and do not constitute 'disguised promotion'.

It is important to realise that this means the majority of activities undertaken by field-based teams fall within the scope of the Code, even though the individuals in some of those teams might consider themselves as operating in a *non*-promotional role.

Potentially, any activity undertaken by (or on behalf of) a pharmaceutical company about prescription medicines could fall within the scope of the Code. This very wide scope reflects the commercial nature of pharmaceutical companies – to provide (and therefore sell) medicines. However, there is a sensible line to be drawn between those activities undertaken in support of a product and those undertaken in support of the company. There is also the need to differentiate between marketing activities and those connected with product development. Differentiating between the various activities and the intent behind them is where things start to get more complicated.

Promotional activities

The ABPI Code applies to any activity that is associated with the prescription of medicines by healthcare professionals in the UK. In the majority of cases, the promotion of over-the-counter (OTC) medicines does not fall within the scope of the ABPI Code. Where the promotion of an OTC medicine is to encourage HCPs to *recommend* that patients *purchase* the medicine, then the activity is covered by the PAGB Professional Code. However, OTC medicines can also be prescribed under certain circumstances. When the aim is to encourage prescriptions, the ABPI Code applies.

The ABPI Code defines promotion as any activity undertaken by a company that promotes the 'prescription, supply, sale, administration, recommendation, or consumption of its medicines'.

- Journal and direct mail advertising
- Many of the activities of representatives
- Material used by representatives
- The supply of medical samples
- The provision of inducements of any kind to prescribe, supply, administer, recommend, buy or sell medicines
- The provision of hospitality for promotional purposes
- The sponsorship of promotional meetings
- The sponsorship of scientific meetings (including travel and accommodation)
- All other conceivable forms of sales promotion
- Innovative pricing arrangements and reimbursements schemes

Non-promotional activities

The Code also covers a number of non-promotional areas. In essence, this means the purpose of the activity is not meant to be directly facilitating increased use of a specific medicine. Many of the activities listed below can easily become promotional, however, if they are conducted inappropriately:

- The publication of clinical trials
- Non-interventional studies
- The provision of information to the public about medicines and diseases
- Market research
- The provision of goods, services and funding in support of the NHS; research; medical education; and patient care
- Interactions with patients and patient groups
- Paying HCPs to provide services to the industry

- Market expansion activities
- Joint Working: partnership working with healthcare organisations
- Information for patients
- The provision of medical samples to healthcare professionals
- Responses to individual (or published) enquiries and comments from HCPs (as long as they relate specifically to the points raised)
- Information related to human health and diseases, as long as there is no direct or indirect reference to specific medicines
- Declarations relating to transfers of value to healthcare professionals and healthcare organisations
- Genuine risk minimisation material as approved by the MHRA (new for 2019)

As part of the marketing authorization process companies can be required to have risk minimisation plans and material approved by the MHRA as part of the company's pharmacovigilance obligations. Such approved documentation is exempt from the definition of promotion and can be delivered by a representative or included on a company website without being considered to be promotion of the medicine to which it refers.

Medical Science Liaisons (MSLs)

Note that a number of points above related to 'representatives'. The definition of 'representative' is very broad and encompasses many individuals who do not have the word 'sales' in their job description. In effect, a representative is anyone who proactively calls on HCPs for the purpose of discussing medicines. This means that the manner in which an MSL works must be carefully considered to ensure that MSLs are not seen as sales representatives when they undertake the proactive elements of the role.

Corporate activities

The Code recognises the fact that pharmaceutical companies are also businesses. In order to *facilitate* the promotion of a product, there is a need to promote the interests of the company. This might, for example, include attracting employees or communicating with financial markets. The Code refers to those activities in support of the *company* as corporate activities. In most instances, corporate activities fall outside the scope of the Code. However, as an MSL, you are unlikely to be involved in such activities.

Of course, in addition to the Code, a pharmaceutical company has to abide by certain rules and regulations that have nothing to do with medicines. When there is a clash between the requirements of the Code and the law, the law takes precedence. That said, the Code stresses compliance with all relevant laws and therefore the circumstances in which clashes occur between the Code and the law should be extremely rare.

Multiple 'hats'

There are times when the customers of pharmaceutical companies perform multiple roles. For example, a doctor might be a prescriber in primary care as well as being the purchaser in a dispensary business. He or she might also be a director within a primary care organisation and an official of a professional society. The same doctor might also be an advisor to a patient group or the owner of a private limited company that provides services to the pharmaceutical industry; in addition, the doctor might also interact with the pharmaceutical company in his or her capacity as a shareholder. Thankfully, the Code recognises that a variety of interactions might occur in different circumstances.

The general rule of thumb is to consider the *intent* of the interaction. It is perfectly acceptable for two friends to meet in the pub for a drink – even if one is an MSL and the other is a GP. What is not acceptable is if an MSL invites someone to the pub *because* they are a GP. In case 2412/7/11 a company employee was accused of inappropriate behaviour because he took a nurse from his territory on holiday with him; it was his wife ...

In case 2749/1/15, difficulties arose because the friendship between a company employee and an HCP was not disclosed within the company. A complaint later alleged that the HCP received consultancy business from the company only because of the existence of the friendship.

Operational boundaries

Under the Code, the UK arm of the pharmaceutical company is responsible for all the activities of all of its employees and all of its agencies, whether they take place in the UK or overseas.

The principle of accountability also extends to co-marketing agreements and partnerships. So if two companies jointly market a product, then any allegation against one is automatically treated as an allegation against both companies individually. The principle of accountability encompasses every conceivable situation in which the company could be linked back to an activity. Nor is ignorance an excuse. Even if the company does not know about the activities of its employees or agents, it is still accountable – this applies even if the MSL acted directly against the company's instructions.

It is also important to consider the Code's geographical reach. There are numerous international meetings each year; many medical journals have an international distribution and readership; as does online content. The potential therefore exists for companies to fall foul of the UK ABPI Code inadvertently when the parent company or an overseas affiliate undertakes activities that impact the UK.

Basically, the UK ABPI Code applies in the following circum-stances:

- if an activity is done by or on behalf of the UK affiliate
- activities organised by any UK-based entity of a pharmaceutical company, including international teams based in the UK
- if the activity occurs on UK soil
- if the company undertakes an activity with a UK HCP – even if the UK company does not know about it
- if the material (e.g. an advertisement) is made available in a UK-based publication
- if material is sent to or targeted at a UK resident
- material generated by an international team based in the UK and released to an audience that includes UK residents

As far as the Code is concerned, 'UK' includes the Channel Islands and the Isle of Man. However, all-Ireland meetings are international events, because, of course, Eire is a distinct country from the UK.

It is also important to note that the UK's PMCPA would also be responsible for ruling on the international activities and materials controlled by international teams based in the UK, even if the EFPIA Code was more applicable than the UK Code.

In case 2940/2/17, Astellas was ruled in breach of the ABPI Code for releasing international materials that contained incorrect prescribing information.

In case 2556/11/12, a number of UK companies were held accountable for the activities of their Eire sister companies for a meeting that was held in Belfast. Even though the meeting was an 'all Ireland' event, it fell within the scope of the (UK) ABPI Code of Practice and the associated hospitality did not meet the requirements of the UK Code. (Eire has its own code and regulatory authority – see www.ipha.ie).

chapter 3

the non-promotional status of an MSL

An increasing number of pharmaceutical companies are employing field-based scientists or medical science liaisons (MSLs). This is an interesting role which poses numerous challenges and complexities. There have been only a handful of Code cases regarding such teams and few have reached conclusions, but there are a couple of cases that help – and the PMCPA's Clause 3 guidance is particularly helpful.

The MSL role takes many guises: they might be called scientists, medical scientists, medical information executives, medical liaison managers, therapy specialists, field-based scientist or a host of other titles.

While the PMCPA recognizes that MSLs undertake a range of activities, a key aspect of the role is to ensure that customers have access to appropriate information about company products. In that sense, for at least that part of the role, they can be regarded as a field-based Medical Information team. Indeed, in some companies, they have been line-managed within the Medical Information department.

A key focus of an MSL's role is the reactive provision of answers to questions (including off-licence product use) from HCPs. This means the MSL should wait for a question from a customer and then visit the customer to provide the answer.

The problem is that there will be peaks and troughs in the workload of such individuals. Unlike sales representatives, MSLs are not supposed to be proactively approaching customers for appointments to discuss product – this would make the call promotional under the Code; under such circumstances, discussion of off-licence information would therefore be a breach of the Code and also a breach of the Medicines Act. However, no company is going to employ a team of field-based people to sit at home and wait for the phone to ring. This introduces the need for MSLs to undertake a variety of proactive tasks in the wider scope of medical liaison.

Care is needed because if a company encourages the customer to ask for information about an unlicensed area, that is the same as promoting off-licence and is regarded as a breach.

It is acceptable for MSLs to write to customers and explain the services they offer. It is inappropriate name a product and seek an appointment to discuss it.

Performance measurement

Another challenge when working with an MSL team is assessing performance. Some form of measurement is essential to be able to prove (or deny) achievement of objectives (and therefore bonus payments) at year-end. The choice of measurement needs to be very carefully considered for scientific teams. Setting an overall call rate for MSLs to achieve and linking it to their personal objectives is inappropriate, as is the establishment of annual activity targets against named target customers. This is because the product-related aspects of the MSL role are reactive – they have absolutely no way of influencing who sees them and how often in relation to product discussions (see case 2987/10/17).

However, it is acceptable for companies to define minimum work standards that they expect individual scientists (or scientist teams) to achieve. For example, responding to requests within a particular time frame; or the ratio of queries answered by letter versus personal visits. Presumably, before the company employs a scientist team, it has already completed an analysis that identifies the need for such a service and how many individuals are required to meet the demand. Therefore, it is appropriate to expect each individual scientist to complete a certain number of visits per day in response to that demand and to monitor the activity (demand) for the service in each geographical location (scientist territory). However, the company should continue to monitor the underlying demand to ensure that the MSLs are not placed in a position where they have to solicit calls in order to reach their expected activity level.

For example, a company may decide that an activity level of less than ten customer visits per week indicates an unsustainable lack of demand for the service, leading to its discontinuation. So, it is appropriate for them to track the actual number of calls made by each MSL over time.

Proactive visits

Other activities that the scientist team can undertake vary between companies.

Anything that involves visiting customers proactively to discuss products is likely to be regarded as a sales call, which has obvious implications. For example, in case 2505/5/12, an MSL role included pro-active calling. The PMCPA indicated that the *concept* was not unacceptable provided two key criteria were met: that the proactive visits were on-licence and that the MSLs sat and passed the Representative Exam. (In effect, the MSLs had become part-time sales representatives!)

However, MSLs might run training sessions on medical conditions and offer these proactively. MSLs could also be involved in discussions regarding the suitability of sites for involvement in clinical trials.

The range of proactive tasks that an MSL can undertake is considerable. The key consideration is that the Code applies to the task and not the role of the individual that undertakes it. This means that proactive visits to discuss a medicine must be regarded as sales calls, regardless of the scientific level of the discussion.

Proactive visits to discuss study publications or to brief a speaker are non-promotional visits that can comfortably be undertaken by an MSL.

Interactions with representatives

MSLs can speak at meetings organized by sales representatives and could, in theory work with a sales representative on an exhibition stand. However, any product discussions must then be within the license.

Some companies allow MSLs to accompany a sales representative on a call so that they can be introduced to the customer concerned. However, in such circumstances the MSL must remember that any discussions in that visit must remain firmly on-label of the relevant product, because the visit is not reactive; and because the sales representative is present.

Some companies ban MSLs from being present at sales conferences when the latest campaign is being presented. This is not necessary, but it is understandable. MSLs do not need to know the promotional messaging for a product; they only need to know the best way to manage customer questions about the product.

In most companies it is regarded as inappropriate for MSLs to discuss the content of their HCP interactions with the local representatives; this is because many of the questions will involve discussion about the off-licence use of the product.

However, MSLs should always be guided by company policy in all these matters.

Bonus structures

There are no hard and fast rules in relation to MSL bonus and reward structures. However, the challenges for Pharma when conducting non-promotional activities are avoiding accusations of disguised promotion or pre-licence promotion; and maintaining credibility.

This means that most MSL reward programmes are related to company performance rather than product performance. If a team claims to be non-promotional but then operates to local sales targets, it must be assumed that their activities and decisions will be swayed by those targets (and associated bonuses).

chapter 4

expected standards

The Code applies to what MSLs say as well as what is written on their technical material. It also applies to all the e-mails and texts that they send. This means that all oral and written communications from MSLs need to meet the usual requirements of being fair, balanced, accurate, etc.

The manner in which MSLs access customers is also carefully controlled.

This brief chapter will therefore provide some examples of the types of activity that breach the high standards expected by the industry – and some examples of activities that have been challenged and deemed to be acceptable.

The clause that no one wants to be accused of breaching is clause 2. A breach of this clause means that the actions of the company have been so bad that they have brought the entire industry into disrepute. Breaches of clause 2 should be rare. A breach might be ruled for multiple transgressions in a short space of time; when patient safety is at risk; for undertaking off-licence promotion; or providing inducements to gain prescriptions.

Clause 9.1 simply states that high standards must be maintained at all times. This is incredibly general and, like clause 2, could encompass almost any inappropriate activity that a company undertakes. Essentially, pharmaceutical companies are expected to set and maintain certain standards regarding the behaviour of their employees. When the guidance and control break down, standards have, by definition, not been maintained.

Both of these clauses are, to a certain extent, vague. This means that activities which do not specifically breach any other clause in the Code can still rate a breach of either (or both) of these two clauses, depending on the circumstances. It may therefore be helpful to look at some examples of the types of activity which have been considered before. Remember, however, that it is often the context and the overall scenario that results in a breach of these three clauses, rather than a single, definable action.

- A company employee arranged for a nurse to undertake a therapy review. However, they failed to follow company procedure and the review was unapproved by the company. Breach of clause 9.1. (Case 2322/5/10)
- A company employee told a hospital consultant that they had not prescribed enough product in return for a donation that had been previously given to the hospital. Breaches of clauses 9.1 and 2, plus the representative was – unsurprisingly – banned from the hospital. (Case 2044/9/07)
- In case 2290/12/09, MSLs attended a dinner the evening prior to an advisory board (breaches clauses 9.1 and 2)
- In case 2783/7/15, a company was ruled in breach of clause 2 for the inappropriate arrangements of an advisory board
- Case 2310/4/10 a speaker presentation was regarded as promotion of an unlicensed medicine because it failed to meet the criteria of scientific exchange (breaches of clauses 9.1 and 2)
- Case 2331/5/09 a medical exhibition stand was regarded as pre-licence promotional activity and ruled in breach of clause 9.1

It should also be remembered that endorsement of a product will be regarded as a promotional statement.

In theory, breaches of both of these major clauses ought to be exceedingly rare. Sadly, there is no shortage of recent examples. The PMCPA actually publishes *advertisements* publicly declaring all cases where clause 2 has been breached. There are also a number of other clauses that deal with standards in general.

Clause 9.2 states that all material and activities should recognise the 'special nature' of medicines. The professional nature of the audience must also be recognised and the material should not cause offence. The standards expected from pharmaceutical companies are higher than those expected from other industries and therefore certain types of behaviour are not acceptable.

References to professionals and professional bodies

As you might expect, this is an area where it is advisable to tread carefully. Securing endorsement from a professional society or key opinion leader about the merits of a product can be incredibly powerful, but it has to be done properly. Equally, any references to organisations or individuals have to be carefully worded so that they do not give the impression that endorsement has been given if it hasn't.

References to other products and companies

To explain the technical properties of a product, it is sometimes necessary to make comparisons with the products of other companies. Comparisons are ok as long as they are fair and balanced. Derogatory comments about a competitor would not be regarded as 'appropriate' (and would be a breach of clause 8.1).

There are, of course, a whole series of rules to follow when making comparisons. The complicated rules regarding the development of clause 7 (information, claims and comparisons), also apply to MSL materials even though these are obviously not meant to be promotional in nature or tone. This is just one reason why most MSL materials are approved by head office prior to being used . . .

For similar reasons, it is not acceptable to use, or reproduce, official documents without permission. So, for example, MSLs could not distribute a copy of NICE guidelines or a PCT formulary unless permission had been sought for that purpose – and after the documents had been reviewed by the company's medical department and formally certified as being completely aligned with the Code.

training requirements

There are four major training and examination requirements specified in the Code:

*   Code training (16.1)
*   Adverse event training (16.2)
*   Disease and product knowledge (15.1)
*   Representative examinations (16.3)

While the latter two bullets are specific to sales representatives, the underlying principles of the clauses do have relevance to MSLs.

As with all areas of the Code, the pharmaceutical company is responsible for its agents and contractors. Contract sales staff must be regularly trained in the Code and in company SOPs.

ABPI Code training

It is a requirement of the Code that all representatives are trained not just on the disease area, but on the Code itself. There is no clear information in the Code about how often people should be trained. Many companies ensure that a refresher on the whole Code is under-taken on an annual basis as an absolute minimum; others ensure that employees are kept informed about the evolving 'case law' as new rulings are published by the PMCPA.

Training resources available from Compliance Hub

*   Summaries of relevant PMCPA rulings
*   Advanced Code courses for experienced staff
*   Basic training on the Code for new employees
*   On-line courses

Companies with a structured training programme are more likely to get a clean bill of health during audits and inspections and are more likely to avoid the more common compliance mistakes.

Pharmacovigilance training

Everyone who works for the company (including contractors) must be trained in the 'relevant pharmacovigilance requirements'. For most people, this means knowing how to recognise and report an adverse event. It is an absolute requirement that companies keep records of pharmacovigilance training.

All adverse events should be reported to the company according to the local SOP – typically calling the pharmacovigillance or medical information team.

"Adverse events" include all side effects experienced with the product (even those that are well documented). However it is also necessary to report instances of off-label use, and where it is known that the product is used during pregnancy and breast feeding.

Product training

MSLs should be able to provide full and accurate information about the medicines they discuss. MSLs therefore need comprehensive training in the product and the relevant disease area.

Many companies seek to make their training as realistic as possible. This involves allowing MSLs and representatives to practice in front of real HCPs who are paid for their time and who give feedback on the employees' performance. In cases 2410/6/11 and 2414/6/11, the activities of two companies were examined to determine whether the overall arrangements represented disguised selling in that HCPs were effectively being paid to listen to product pitches! Thankfully, common sense prevailed. It was decided that using HCPs in such training sessions were acceptable as long as the HCPs were chosen at random or in a manner unrelated to sales potential, and as long as the remuneration was proportionate to the time spent on the activity.

ABPI representatives examination

All sales representatives must pass the relevant ABPI representative examination.

For clarity, Medical Sales Liaisons (MSLs) do **not** normally need to sit the representative examination. However, in case 2505/5/12, it was identified that when MSLs undertake some proactive calling on HCPs in connection with discussions on medicines, *that part* of the MSL role is considered as promotional activity; in that instance, the individuals concerned would need to sit the exam as they then (in effect) have a dual role.

However, it is also worth being aware that in case 2306/3/10, the Panel made a reference to the fact that "development of relationships" might constitute a promotional activity. In this instance the inference was that generic sales representatives whose duties included developing relationships might no longer be considered to be dealing solely with price and might need to upgrade their examination status.

chapter 6

behind the scenes (approval of material)

Every company nominates an individual who retains ultimate responsibility for compliance with the Code. This is assumed to be the managing director.

The managing director assigns responsibility for the approval of material used by the MSL team to Signatories whose role is to ensure that the requirements of the Code are met.

Certification and examination

The Signatories ensure that all promotional material and activities are formally certified as being compliant with the Code of Practice. The Signatories must literally sign a certificate to confirm that they have assessed the material or activity and determined that it is compliant with the Code, the Marketing Authorisation and the relevant advertising regulations and that it is a 'fair and truthful representation of the facts about the medicine'.

Field-based employees must therefore never use or distribute any material unless it has been formally approved by head office or is created in line with the process for answering reactive medical information enquiries. Head office approval is usually indicated by the presence of a 'date of preparation' and an identifying code number on the item (even the non- promotional material).

Examples of materials and activities that should be approved by head office:

- MSL slide decks
- Sales material

- Disease awareness campaigns
- Reference material about diseases and products
- Educational material about medicines and diseases intended for the public
- Agreements with patient groups (MSLs should not make contact directly with patient groups without prior head office approval)
- Anything and everything connected with 'services to medicine'
- Training material for representatives on the technical aspects of medicines
- Briefings for representatives about how to sell those medicines
- Instructions on call rates and bonus structures
- Campaign briefings to representatives
- Logistics and arrangements for international meetings

It is worth noting that all meetings must also comply with the Code, even if they are not submitted to head office for approval (the approval procedures for meetings vary greatly between companies). Most companies delegate the approval of the arrangements for local meetings to the local team, dependent on the budget and the circumstances. An MSL might therefore self-approve the arrangements for a medical meeting, but the MSL must be sure that the arrangements comply with the Code and with company policy.

Technical material and Obligatory information

There is a certain amount of obligatory information that must be provided on just about all product-related material that is provided proactively to customers. Material that is provided reactively does not require the obligatory information under the Code, but many companies add it anyway …

Obligatory information includes:

- Generic name
- Black triangle
- The date the material was prepared
- A unique identifying number
- Adverse event reporting statement
- Prescribing Information (PI)

These are just some of the things that Signatories check when reviewing material. They also have to consider whether all the content is in line with the product licence and whether the information is fair and balanced.

Part of the material review process includes an appraisal of the validity of the material and all the information it contains. Of course, it is both the intention behind the material and the use to which it is put that combine to determine whether it is acceptable. In general, anything provided proactively which contains the name of a medicine should be regarded as promotional and reviewed as such. However, the vast majority of 'rules' that apply to promotional material also apply to non-promotional material – and to what is said verbally by MSLs and speakers. The structure and context of sentences are crucial in avoiding breaches.

Statements about medicines and medical conditions must be

- Accurate
- Balanced
- Fair
- Objective
- Unambiguous
- Based on an up-to-date evaluation of all the evidence

Statements must not mislead, directly or indirectly by

- Distortion
- Exaggeration
- Undue emphasis

It is also important to realise that the inadvertent inclusion of a promotional claim can render an entire project promotional, even if the original intent was not a promotional one. This includes the provision of general information, replies to enquiries and comparisons with other products. The content of clinical papers is regarded as promotional if those papers are issued proactively by an MSL and must therefore be consistent with the Code. Be aware that it is not necessary for the brand name to be present for a statement to be considered 'promotional'.

Representative Briefings

On occasion, MSLs will be asked to train sales representatives. All such briefings given to representatives must in themselves comply with the Code, and be certified by registered head office signatories.

Certified briefing instructions are required for all information issued about the company's medicines – and all instructions about how to promote those medicines.

It should also be noted that presentations at sales conferences, teleconferences, local team meetings, sharing best practice and emails from MSLs to sales representatives about products should all be regarded as 'briefings'.

investigating breaches of the Code, undertakings and returning material

Investigating an alleged breach

Try as we might to maintain high standards, the very nature of the Code means that we will disagree with competitors (and sometimes customers) about the 'right' way to do something. The disagreement might be about a fundamental interpretation of a key principle or it might be a finely balanced technical point. Regardless of the subject, the person who raised the complaint feels strongly enough to put pen to paper and therefore it is right and proper that the concerns are investigated.

In theory, the process for managing Code complaints is very straight-forward. Someone complains. The PMCPA writes to the company that is alleged to have done wrong. The company submits material that explains what happened. The PMCPA makes a ruling. The error is corrected.

But, of course, nothing is that simple! Indeed, the time involved in establishing the facts about what happened is considerable and the actual exchange of information can be just as burdensome.

Inter-company dialogue

Where two companies disagree about material or activities, the Code mandates that they must try to resolve their disagreement privately first. This is essentially to avoid 'public slanging matches'. It also means that some concerns can be resolved very quickly and amicably with little more than a phone call and a follow-up letter.

Where companies cannot resolve the matter through dialogue, a formal complaint is made to the Prescription Medicines Code of Practice Authority – the PMCPA.

The PMCPA manages all complaints for companies that are members of the ABPI and those that agree to abide by its Code. Where a complaint is lodged against a company that will not submit to the jurisdiction of the PMCPA, the complainant is advised to contact the MHRA directly. In most instances, companies would rather have their case heard by the PMCPA.

Complaints can be received from any pharmaceutical company, healthcare professional, patient, member of the public or employee of any pharmaceutical company – in fact, just about anyone. Complaints can even be made anonymously, although the weighting placed behind evidence submitted this way is often lower because it is difficult to verify. Criticism of a company in the media is automatically taken up by the PMCPA Director as per the constitution. There is also an agreement between the MHRA and PMCPA so that complaints are referred from one to the other based on the nature of the allegation.

The names of complainants from outside the industry are kept confidential. With the complainant's permission, his or her name might be released to the company in order to carry out a detailed investigation. Anonymous complaints can be a boon and a blessing. It is possible that the PMCPA will not be able to ask the complainant further questions. It is also possible that the information provided in the complaint will be insufficient for the company to investigate fully.

Once the PMCPA receives a valid complaint, it has the authority to request copies of all relevant material from the relevant pharmaceutical company, including copies of the relevant approval certificates. The voluntary nature of the Code places the burden of honesty directly on the member company. Cynics might say this enables the company being investigated to hide incriminating evidence. However, breaches of this trust are taken extremely seriously and have historically been responsible for companies being suspended from ABPI membership.

Once the company receives notification of a complaint, it has 10 working days to submit a response. If the complaint is received from the MHRA and it relates to a patient safety matter, the response time may be reduced to five working days.

Rulings are based on the evidence provided in the allegation and the information provided by the defendant. Once a decision has been reached, the complainant and the respondent are advised of the ruling. Both have the right to appeal the decision. Appeals are made in person at a formal meeting of the Appeal Board, usually held monthly.

Material that is ruled in breach must be withdrawn. In certain cases, usually those connected with patient safety, the PMCPA may ask for the material to be withdrawn as soon as the complaint is lodged or at any time during the investigation.

Once a breach is ruled, the respondent company has five working days to submit a formal undertaking that the material will be withdrawn. Companies are expected to take all possible steps to comply with an undertaking.

When the case is completed, the respondent company must pay an administration fee for each separate breach. If no breach is ruled and the complaint is from a pharmaceutical company, it is the complainant who must pay the administration fee. Administration fees are around £5000 and are higher if the case is taken to appeal.

(Non-ABPI members pay higher administration fees than members, who have already contributed to the running costs of the PMCPA.)

- Audit of procedures and policies
- Pre-vetting of all promotional material
- Public reprimand
- Issuing a corrective statement (i.e. a letter of apology)
- Recovery of in-breach material (including any payments made to customers in connection with the project)
- Removal from the list of non-member companies subject to the jurisdiction of the Authority
- Suspension or expulsion from the ABPI

The details of all complaints are later published. This is important to the principles of transparency.

Sources of information when responding to Code complaints might include:

- Job bags
- Employee briefing documents
- Company policies

- Customer records
- Clinical papers and other references
- Employee emails
- Interviews

Undertaking

The undertaking must be signed by the managing director (or on the MD's behalf by a nominated individual with their authority). The undertaking must include:

- A declaration that the in-breach material or activity has immediately ceased
- A declaration that all possible steps are being taken to prevent a similar breach
- The details of the actions taken by the company to implement the undertaking
- The date on which the in-breach material was last used or the in- breach activity last occurred.

Companies must openly advise their employees when they have been found in breach of the Code. The announcement should refer to the fact of the breach and state clearly which materials have been affected. Instructions should be given to employees as to how materials should be returned or destroyed.

Recalling material

There are principally two reasons why a company would have a recall process. The first is to support the routine changeover of promotional (and non-promotional) material at the end of each campaign cycle. This helps ensure that the material used by representatives is as current as possible. The second is to remove material from circulation following a breach (or to honour an agreement reached during inter-company dialogue).

In theory, companies should be withdrawing and replacing material on a regular basis. Materials and projects have a maximum two-year 'shelf life' before requiring re-approval; it is rare that material is re- approved owing to changes to PI or new data. It is also a fundamental principle of the Code that any material which has been ruled 'in breach' must be withdrawn from use immediately. Continuing to use material once it has been ruled in breach is regarded as a very serious matter indeed and the lengths to which companies are expected to go are considerable.

While it is understandable that the routine changeover of promotional material might be handled in a slightly more relaxed manner, it is probably beneficial to have similar processes for the two types of material withdrawal. It is not uncommon for representatives to store significant quantities of campaign material and it would be relatively easy for items from a previous campaign to be inadvertently used again.

Following a breach of the Code (or the Medicines Act), companies give an undertaking to the PMCPA (or MHRA) that all material containing the offending phrases will be withdrawn from circulation. A breach of this undertaking is regarded as extremely serious and almost always results in the company being ruled in breach of clause 2 as well. These days, breaches of clause 2 are usually subject to public reprimand and advertisements in the professional press.

Routine withdrawal of campaign materials

No company wants old material in circulation. Sometimes material is withdrawn to refresh the campaign, or to strengthen or realign promotional claims, in line with the new marketing strategy.

Whenever material is approved it has a maximum 'shelf life' of two years. At the end of this time, material is reassessed to determine its suitability for an extended period of use or must be removed from circulation.

Recall following a breach

On occasion, it is necessary to recall material following an inter-company agreement or a ruling from the PMCPA.

Given the seriousness of a breach of undertaking, it is appropriate that all actions taken when implementing a regulatory recall should be formally documented and archived. Companies are expected to take all possible steps to comply with an undertaking and the list of actions to take into account is a long one! Documentary evidence must be collected from every relevant employee and agency, confirming that they have complied with the recall.

Given the seriousness of a breach of undertaking, it is appropriate that all actions taken when implementing a regulatory recall should be formally documented and archived. Companies are expected to take all possible steps to comply with an undertaking and the list of actions to take into account is a long one! Documentary evidence must be collected from every relevant employee and agency, confirming that they have complied with the recall.

The recall of materials at the request of a regulatory authority should take precedence over all other company activities, except

patient safety. It is essential that MSLs follow the instructions very carefully and return, or destroy, every single item of in-breach material. Returning material to a central point allows the company to confirm that the items in question have actually been destroyed.

Inadequate action leading to a breach of the undertaking is likely to be regarded as bringing discredit to the industry and ruled as a breach of clause 2.

section 2

meetings

chapter 8

meeting principles

Overview

Pharmaceutical companies undertake a very wide range of events and meetings. Some are deliberately promotional; others strictly scientific. They might be either organised or sponsored by the company. The event might equally be one of collaboration between a company and a professional society. This chapter seeks to provide some general guidance for all meetings and then chapter 9 investigates the unique characteristics of different types of event.

The structure of these chapters is intended to help the reader identify the relevant aspects of what can be a huge and complicated subject:

- General principles
- Justification for the meeting (agenda)
- Location
- Hospitality (Accommodation & meal costs)
- Attendees.

General principles

Regardless of the detail, all meetings policies say roughly the same things: make sure that education is the main focus of the meeting. Choose a business-like venue and don't spend too much on food or alcohol. Don't disguise any promotional activities and don't include off-licence subjects in promotional meetings. Keep control of the meeting.

The majority of meetings principles apply regardless of whether the meeting is organised by the company or the company is merely providing sponsorship; Pharma's involvement in any capacity renders the meeting liable to some aspects of the Code. Companies should apply the same considerations to meetings that are sponsored as they would to those that the company organises.

Company policies are also typically stricter than the Code itself. This is usually to avoid long drawn- out debates about each and every event so that organisers can operate within guidelines that allow the company to manage risk whilst allowing front-line employees to get on with the day job quickly and easily.

Attracting delegates to the meeting

The only inducement you are allowed to offer to get people to attend your meeting is the quality of the agenda!

With the exception of speakers and advisors, it is not acceptable to pay delegates to attend an educational meeting. This rule extends to journalists, healthcare professionals and all other delegates.

It is not acceptable to pay money for locums to cover the work of those who attend meetings.

General points that apply to all meetings

There are core requirements that apply to all meetings:

- There must be clear educational content
- The venue must be appropriate
- Subsistence must be of an appropriate level
- Only relevant HCPs (and appropriate administrative personnel) can attend the meeting
- Only relevant HCPs (and appropriate administrative personnel) can receive hospitality from the company
- The extent of the company's involvement must be clearly stated
- Delegates must not be paid to attend

Companies can organise or sponsor a very wide range of events. However, the one thing that they all have in common is that they all have to comply with the Code. Healthcare professionals are, of course, free to organise and pay for their own events. However, pharmaceutical companies can only provide support if the arrangements for the meeting comply with the Code. The company employee in attendance is always responsible for the company's compliance with the Code.

Companies are also able to set up or sponsor meetings jointly with other companies. Where this is the case, all parties are jointly liable for the meeting – however, each company is, of course, individually responsible for the content of their exhibition stands.

Regardless of the type of meeting or who organised it, all the documentation must clearly state the nature of the involvement of the pharmaceutical company. For example, it might say that the event is organised by the company, or that the company has provided an educational grant towards the general running costs, or that the company has funded the travel costs of a particular speaker. It might also be the case that the meeting is 'organised in partnership between' the company and a professional society. Whatever the arrangements, the statement must be clear about the role the company has played in setting up or supporting the event.

Examples of meeting types

- Rep-led meetings in general practices or hospital departments to promote their products
- Exhibition stands at postgraduate meetings or medical society conferences
- MSL presentations to hospital departments meetings
- Scientific congresses and symposia
- Management training courses
- Meetings of clinical trialists
- Patient support group meetings
- Company 'stand alone' international meetings
- Meetings in connection with Joint Working projects

It is not acceptable for companies to sponsor or provide entertainment. Many independent congresses and medical society meetings provide some form of entertainment to their delegates and the fact that *some* social activities take place is not normally a reason for Pharma to avoid the event altogether. However, if companies have concerns about the extent or type of social arrangements at a meeting, then they should withdraw from supporting it altogether because of the 'overall impression' created by the sponsorship.

Agenda

The agenda is the justification for the meeting. The meeting must be educational in the sense that the delegates should learn something relevant to the practice of medicine, etc). This applies regardless of whether the meeting is *organised* by the company, or *sponsored* by it. However, those two points are not the whole story; and neither are they completely straightforward.

To be valid under the Code, the attendees have to learn something that is relevant to the way they perform their role (e.g. management skills or medical knowledge). Companies should also consider the relevance of agenda topics to UK medical practice, so a presentation about the challenges of medical practice in the Sahara Desert might be fascinating, but it is unlikely to be relevant to UK medical practice and is therefore unsuitable for Pharma sponsorship.

For proactively organised meetings, the agenda topics and presentations must be within the relevant product licence. It is not acceptable to structure the agenda in such a way that the delegates are left with the impression that a product can be used for an off-label indication. Another example, would be that it is perfectly acceptable for a company which sells a product for schizophrenia to offer places at meetings about schizophrenia. However, if the product licence does not cover other conditions, it would usually be inappropriate to organise a meeting on a wider range of psychiatric disorders unless head office applied specific rules to it.

There are of course many occasions when off-licence use of a product might be referred to by delegates and speakers at an independent meeting sponsored by a pharmaceutical company. However, companies should avoid committing support for meetings where it is obvious that a significant part of the agenda is on a topic that is off-licence for their products.

Location/ venue

This is typically the area that causes representatives (and compliance officers) the most stress. The Code does not allow the use of 'lavish', 'extravagant' or 'deluxe' venues. However, it declines to define what these terms mean. The Code does not specifically ban the use of five- star hotels, for example, but many companies have chosen to ban them anyway. This is because the determination of what is 'lavish' is purely subjective and depends on the individual circumstances at the time. A venue that might be appropriate for an all-day meeting of hospital chief executives may not be suitable for a regular evening gathering of local GPs. The risk is also higher when an overnight stay is involved.

So what defines 'acceptability'? The star rating is one measure. Cost is, of course, another. However, there are occasions when it is possible to secure a discount that makes a five-star venue less expensive than a four-star one. Bear in mind that the impression created is more important than the actual cost.

What the Code actually says is that meetings must be held in 'appropriate venues conducive to the main purpose of the event'. In essence, what that means is that the venue should be chosen for its logistical facilities, not as the attraction for people to attend. However, the supplementary information to this clause) also specifies the need to avoid venues 'renowned for their leisure facilities'.

Because the media have highlighted the activities of some pharmaceutical companies over the past few years, there is a trend towards being more cautious than the Code requires and to consider only the external impression created by the use of certain venues, regardless of the logistical merits of the choice. Effectively, this means that hotels that contain certain leisure facilities (such as spas and golf courses) may be out of bounds, even though the meeting agenda does not allow any time to actually use the facilities. There has not been a recent case that ruled on the use of a four-star hotel with a golf course being used as the venue for an evening meeting and as long as the rationale was clearly documented, it would *probably* be OK. However, few companies are willing to take the chance when there are numerous other options that carry a lower risk.

There is also a popular belief that all sports grounds are

completely banned under the Code. This is untrue. However, once again, impression is important. There is a difference between using the conference facilities in a football stadium and encouraging customers to attend the meeting because it is held at the home of a famous football club!

There are therefore some general rules of thumb that can be applied, which will help keep the choice of venue appropriate. (See the box for guidance on overall planning for meetings.) .

If you are worried that a particular venue might not be acceptable, you have two choices – ask a Signatory for advice; or choose somewhere else. If the high-profile venue is your last resort, then it is probably acceptable to use it (as long as you document the other places you have tried). The key is to make sure that the rationale for using any venue is fully documented. No rationale: no defence.

- Avoid five-star hotels
- Avoid spa resorts
- Avoid venues with golf courses
- Avoid sporting venues
- Avoid venues owned by famous chefs
- Avoid restaurants with numerous Michelin stars and AA rosettes
- Choose a venue that is central for all delegates and easy to access
- Never put a photograph of the venue on the invitation
- Never list the venue's leisure facilities on the invitation
- Always book a private room for the meeting

Avoid five-star hotels. While the Code does not ban them specifically, it is difficult to find one that would not be described as 'lavish', 'extravagant' or 'deluxe' (and most company policies ban them anyway). The vast majority of four-star business hotels have good quality meeting facilities. Most airport hotels are OK because they are designed for business meetings and overnight visits (rather than venues designed to attract guests for extended stays with, say, extensive leisure facilities).

Avoid spa resorts. Note that there is a difference between a 'spa resort' and a hotel that might have a single massage room. Many company policies draw the line by excluding any hotel that has even a single spa treatment room. Fitness centres and gyms are, of course, OK.

Avoid venues with golf courses. This is all about perception. Historically, representatives sponsored doctors' golf afternoons and joined them on the green; the historical perceptions persist, so any venue with a golf course is likely to be frowned upon by most signatories.

Avoid venues owned by famous chefs. If you choose a venue for its appropriate location and facilities, and it just happens to have a famous owner, then that's fine. But it is not acceptable to choose it because it has a famous owner. Similarly, certain venues are renowned for being regularly frequented by famous personalities. So to avoid being accused of choosing the venue for that reason, don't go there for business – use it for your team's Christmas party instead.

Avoid restaurants with numerous Michelin stars and AA rosettes. It is appropriate that you provide subsistence to your guests. However, the subsistence is supposed to be secondary to the agenda, so while it is obviously important that the food is edible (and well presented), there is no need to seek out a venue that has won multiple awards.

Choose a venue that is central for all delegates and easy to access. Where does it make more sense to hold a meeting? In a hotel that is just off a major access road in the middle of the MSL territory or a remote country manor that is 30 minutes' drive from the nearest dual carriageway down twisting country lanes that require a sat-nav to negotiate? Remote locations should always be a trigger for compliance teams to look more closely at the arrangements for the event.

Never put a photograph of the venue on the invitation. You are choosing the venue for its facilities. The delegates are visiting it because of the educational content of the agenda. If you add photographs, it starts to look as though you are enticing them to your meeting because it is somewhere 'a bit special'. Similarly, you should not include a picture of the way meals are presented because the food is supposed to be secondary to the educational content. For clarity, it is of course, acceptable to include a map of the location.

Never list the venue's leisure facilities on the invitation. There is no need. Delegates are coming for the education – in that context, they don't need to know about the leisure facilities.

Always book a private room. The public cannot be present during educational meetings organised (or sponsored) by pharmaceutical companies, so it is essential that the meeting takes place in a private area. You also need to be careful that the public cannot see into the room from the outside.

Room hire: there are no firm guidelines regarding the amount of payment that is acceptable. Basically, you pay the going rate for the venue you use. However, there are two occasions when you are not allowed to pay for the hire of a room:

1) You may not pay a GP for the hire of a room within their practice. This is expressly forbidden within the Code.
2) You should also not normally pay hospital departments for the hire of a room. This is more difficult to manage, however, and it has become accepted practice in some hospital departments that in instead of providing sandwiches (or even in addition to providing them), the representative makes a contribution to the department's education fund. The problem with this is that the room is not owned by the department; it is owned by the hospital. So the department doesn't have the right to charge for the use of the room. Regardless of what the money is used for, the HCPs are effectively seeking a payment to attend your meeting. This is unacceptable. If, however, the *hospital management* decides that it is appropriate to charge all representatives a fee for the use of the site's meeting rooms, then of course the situation changes and it would become appropriate to pay a fee for room hire; what is not acceptable is if the department decides independently to generate funds from the 'drug lunch'.

Hospitality

Since the agenda is the *only* thing allowed to entice people to attend a meeting, the *menu* should become a secondary issue. Which is why the Code says that the hospitality must be secondary to the main purpose of the meeting and that the level of subsistence should not be out of proportion to the occasion or exceed the amount that delegates would normally pay for themselves. Most companies have guidance on how much it is acceptable to spend on entertaining guests. The Code itself does not specify any specific limits. However, it is very clear that 'hospitality' is limited to 'subsistence'.

Interpreting this guidance into specific amounts of pounds and pence is not a simple task. Yet it isn't really that difficult to draw some rough 'rules of thumb'.

The reason you are allowed to feed and water the delegates is because in attending your meeting, they may miss a meal or they may require some nourishment. The meal cannot be used as the *attraction* to attend; therefore, it is not necessary (or appropriate) to spend excessively on the food and drink.

Meal costs

Absolute maximum
The Code defines a maximum limit for any individual meal provided as hospitality to an HCP. This has been set at £75 and is regarded as a level that should only be reached under exceptional circumstances. The amount includes drinks but excludes VAT.

Dinner
Most evening meals should be in the £45-£60 price range. In a main- stream restaurant, a typical main course is around £15 to £25. A starter can add up to £10; dessert up to another £10, and coffee around £3-5. This means that the vast majority of meals should be affordable within a £45 – £50 per head budget (inc VAT). Then add around £10 per person for a glass of wine and some soft drinks.

A dinner that costs more than £60 per head is therefore likely to be regarded as excessive. In fact, in most restaurants that would be acceptable under the Code, a three-course meal, coffee and a glass of wine should be achievable for under £50.

There are always arguments about higher prices in certain parts of the country, especially London, and some companies allow for higher costs in major cities. However, in general, if a meal costs over £60 per head (excluding wine) in any city, then as a compliance officer, I would be looking extremely closely at the justification and at the alternative venues that might have been available.

Lunch

Most companies allow around £25 per head for a sit-down lunch or buffet and around £10-15 per head for sandwiches. It is difficult to see how these limits can be exceeded without some considerable effort.

Breakfast

£10-25 per head seems sensible, depending on the location although there is not a lot of 'case precedent' about breakfast meetings.

Wine and alcohol

Usually around £20 per bottle, allowing for up to half a bottle per person. However, this is very dependent on company policy regarding alcohol and in most cases a single glass of house wine is sufficient. And remember that this is only a guideline. It's also a brave (or foolhardy) meeting organiser that lets the delegates choose the wine ... It is usually best to ask the waiters *not* to leave the bottles on the table but to retain control of the bottles and to refill the guests' glasses for them. Waiters are usually experienced in managing the flow of alcohol and can help you make sure that nobody exceeds the drink-drive limits. Even if your guests are staying overnight, the wrong impression can be created if you allow them to drink excessively; what they do in the bar afterwards with their own money is their own concern!

Case precedent

Some insight can be gleaned from case 2084/1/08. The Panel considered that the hospitality (particularly the drinks bill) was on the outer limits of acceptability. The drinks bill was £442 for 42 healthcare professionals plus two representatives (i.e. £10 per head for drinks – including the bar bill and wine with the meal).The Panel expressed their concern about the actual bar bill as well, which was £230 (approx £5 per person), commenting that it seemed excessive given that water and wine were provided on the table (half a bottle of wine per person was provided). The total cost per head for drinks and food was under £40. No breaches were ruled because there were significant delays between courses (presumably owing to problems with restaurant staff levels) and the Panel took this into account, but even taking this into account, the Panel still felt the need to express their concern about the hospitality provided.

There are few companies whose expenses policy still allows wine at lunchtime. It is acceptable to drink wine instead of beer. However, shots and spirits are not appropriate.

It is also necessary to consider the duty of care we owe to our delegates. Providing additional alcohol when someone is already tipsy would clearly be inapproproriate.

Soft drinks

I have yet to meet a Signatory who would refuse to sign off expenses that exceeded the limit because of the quantity of *soft* drinks consumed by delegates. Of course, if you have chosen a venue where a Pepsi is £10 per glass, then you are probably in the wrong venue to start with.

Gala dinners

It is acceptable for representative to attend conference dinners, but not gala dinners. The case precedent relates to an all-Ireland meeting that involved 10 pharmaceutical companies sponsoring a medical society meeting. The meeting included two evening dinners; one was the conference dinner with a meal that was deemed to be within the hospitality limits. The Panel deemed it acceptable for representatives to attend the conference dinner. However, on the second evening was a Gala Dinner with hospitality that was outside the Code's limits; this was deemed to be unacceptable. The conclusion that it is acceptable is for representatives to eat with doctors in the evening during a conference, as long as the meal and venue, etc, are Code compliant. However, remember that company policy may be stricter than the Code.

Speakers

See the chapter on 'engagement of consultants' regarding the selection and contracting of speakers and chairpersons.

Different companies follow different policies regarding whether the slides used by speakers need head office approval. It is clear that companies are responsible for what their speakers say at meetings. Given that the company has organised the meeting, that the speaker is being paid by the company to speak, and that the talk will undoubtedly include some reference to the company's products, it is difficult to argue that the meeting falls outside the Code's definition of 'promotion'.

However the sheer logistics involved in approving every slide set for every speaker is daunting and the challenge of getting speakers to submit slides in time for them to be reviewed is a near-impossibility, let alone the company having the signatory resource capable of reviewing all the presentations. Companies approach this challenge in a variety of ways. Some pre-approve core slide sets that speakers are obliged to use. Others attempt to review all slides sets produced by the speakers in the conscious knowledge that it is not always possible.

A more common approach is to ensure that speakers are properly briefed about their responsibilities under the Code. A verbal briefing is reinforced with written guidance. This mitigates the likelihood of any issues arising (but not the responsibility of the company).

There are a few other points worth bearing in mind. Since companies are responsible for what their speakers say, organisers should be aware of the views of their speakers before inviting them to speak. This means that particularly outspoken speakers might best be avoided.

When arranging meetings, it should be remembered that the vast majority of communications between representatives and health care professionals are subject to the Code. This includes all letters and e-mails that are concerned with recruiting and briefing speakers. Speakers can include company employees, as long as this is clearly stated on the agenda and invitations.

Attendees

Basically, as long as the delegate is a healthcare professional, then everything should be OK. Some non-healthcare professionals can also attend meetings that Pharma organises. Depending on the agenda, it is acceptable for 'relevant decision makers' to attend meetings where you are discussing your products. It is not typically appropriate to have receptionists in the room when promoting products. Social workers are not healthcare professionals, by the way.

Remember as well that you are only allowed to provide subsistence to those who attend the meeting. In other words, you cannot provide catering for the receptionists and secretaries if they have not attended the meeting; and they won't be allowed to attend most of the meetings owing to the subject matter.

It is not appropriate to cater for those whom you know will not be attending the meeting.

Accompaniment by family members

Only HCPs and 'relevant decision makers' can attend medical meetings that are organised or sponsored by Pharma.

In theory, the Code allows for the sponsorship of meetings in which families join the HCPs for the social programme. In practice, companies should consider their position on this very carefully.

Clearly, any exhibition stands must be kept out of sight of the non- HCPs; and partners cannot, of course, attend the educational sessions. But companies are also forbidden from subsidising any costs incurred by family members. How then to clearly identify the costs attributable to the HCP and those attributable to their partner? And bearing in mind that the primary focus of any meeting has to be educational, how to be sure about the true purpose of the event in the first place. Was it education with a social programme tacked on? Or was it designed to be a social event whereby education sessions were added to justify the approach to pharmaceutical companies in an attempt to get financial support? Remember that whilst we may trust the declarations from our customers about the arrangements, Pharma is subject to external scrutiny and audit and we must be able to prove that everything was appropriate.

Companies should therefore bear in mind the challenges of such arrangements:

- Delegates must meet the costs of their personal expenses and all additional costs arising from the fact that another person is staying with them. In practice, it can be difficult to separate the costs involved.
- Delegates may miss some business sessions or subsistence meals and spend time with their guest.
- Some regional societies have very active social agendas accompanying the educational sessions.
- The overall impression created by accompaniment may not be positive.
- Companies should not actively *encourage* or *facilitate* delegates to be accompanied by family members.

chapter 9

considerations for different types of meeting

Company-organised meetings

Depending on the nature of the event, meetings organised by MSLs might be regarded by the Code as promotional or non-promotional. This distinction is important. Meetings that are proactively organised by the company will typically be regarded under the Code as promotional events if product is discussed. This means they should be within the terms of the relevant product licence. In fact, it is very rarely acceptable to discuss products outside the licensed indication at any meeting organised by a company. Company SOPs should always be followed to ensure the appropriate criteria are followed if there is a need to share data about the unlicensed use of a medicine at a company meeting.

Representative meetings

Lunchtime representative meetings are regarded as promotional activities. Rep-organised speaker meetings are generally regarded as promotional activities. This means that if an MSL speaks at a meeting organised by a representative, the entire talk must be within the licensed indication.

Agendas for meetings

Every meeting must have a clearly stated educational purpose and should be supported by appropriate documentation. This typically means providing a written agenda to the department manager in advance of the event – even for short lunchtime meetings.

The topic of most meetings must be within the terms of the

product licence. It is important that the documentation does not mislead the attendees about the purpose of the meeting; promotional content is regarded as educational because it is expected that the attendees learn something about the product. Care should also be taken that a professional impression is given by all the supporting documents. For example, innovative meeting titles can sometimes cause unintended offence.

The agenda and the content must also be tailored to the audience. It would typically be inappropriate for administrative staff to attend meetings that included discussion on a company product unless the content had been specifically tailored to make it relevant to their role. It would be expected that specialists and generalists might receive different presentations.

All documentation relating to planning and implementing company-led meetings are regarded as promotional items under the Code if they contain the name of the product and therefore require formal approval. This includes agendas, invitations, letters and e-mails. It is acceptable to use standard templates that have been approved by company signatories for local completion. However, if handouts are to be used, these require specific certification by the signatories prior to the meeting.

Medical meetings
It may be acceptable for the MSL to make a presentation to a group of HCPs in response to a written request from senior HCP. Under such circumstances, the presentation might include data which is outside the licensed indication of the product. Great care must be taken to present only the data that has been requested. The actual product license must always be clearly stated.

Venues for meetings
It is usually the case that lunchtime meetings occur within healthcare premises. Where this is not the case, the venue should be close to the surgery or hospital and the entire meeting must take place within the alternative venue; it is not advisable to hold the presentation in one venue and go somewhere else for the meal.

Nor is it acceptable to 'bank' the meal – e.g. a lunchtime meeting cannot be followed by an evening meal. An educational meeting and a subsistence meal separated in time are regarded as two separate events.

Sponsored meetings

While MSLs in some companies might not normally be involved in the sponsorship of independent meetings, it is important that MSLs are aware of the criteria that should be applied. In general, all meetings which are sponsored by a pharmaceutical company are expected to attain the same standards as those organised directly by the company itself. The agenda, venue, costs and attendees must all be carefully considered. Similar standards of hospitality should be applied to sponsored and company-organised meetings. This includes costs for accommodation and subsistence. Whilst the organisers have the right to run the meeting in any way they choose, the company has the right to decline the opportunity to sponsor the event.

This means that companies should consider the overall impression given by their sponsorship of an event. Organisers should be made aware of the need for all meeting arrangements, including presentation content, to be in line with the principles of the Code. This means that companies should carefully check the agenda and other documents to ensure that they give a professional impression of the event and the company's involvement. For example, meals should reflect their status as 'subsistence', rather than giving the impression of a 'gala dinner'.

Applications for sponsorship should be accompanied by the agenda, information pertaining to the venue, a breakdown of the costs and a description of the audience type. The company may ask for further information before making a final decision.

Where the content may place the company's (or industry's) reputation at risk, or would not meet the terms of the Code or its policy, the opportunity for sponsorship should be declined. This is why it is completely inappropriate for companies to agree support without first having reviewed the agenda. Where meetings are planned some months in advance, it is understandable that support might be offered before the *detailed* agenda is available. However, support should not be confirmed until the company is sure that the agenda meets the standards of the Code.

It is possible to separate the social and educational aspects of a third-party meeting when considering sponsorship, however it is very difficult to achieve in practice.

Companies are understandably reluctant to approach organisations when they have concerns about the arrangements of meetings they have been asked to support. Such caution and respect is understandable and appropriate: the organisers have the right to do whatever they want at their own meeting. However, pharmaceutical companies have the right to decide whether or not to provide funding. Long term, successful partnerships are not well served by avoiding difficult issues. And HCPs are (usually) very receptive to comments and feedback – after all, they need the sponsorship to enable the meetings to take place.

Note that there is no requirement in the Code for companies to review the slides of speakers at meetings that they *sponsor*. On occasion, a company is invited to pay for or provide a speaker for a session at a sponsored third-party meeting and then it may be appropriate to review the slides – head office will always provide guidance on this point.

Many requests are received for sponsorship of meetings whose content does not fit the traditional mould of medical education. Most companies will not typically sponsor topics such as: team-building events, IT training courses, departmental business or strategy meetings, award ceremonies, and profit generation from practice-based commissioning.

All meetings sponsored by Pharma must bear a declaration of the nature of the company's involvement prominently on all the documentation. In practice, some invitations are issued prior to companies being approached for sponsorship. Under such circumstances, sponsorship should be declared from the point at which the agreement was reached. However, companies should also check that, regardless of which specific company provided support, the delegates had always been aware that Pharma sponsorship was to be sought. For example, the agenda might state that a pharmaceutical exhibition is taking place, or bear a declaration that 'the meeting is being supported by the pharmaceutical industry'.

Remember that any funding contributed to support a meeting (except food) falls within the scope of disclosure. Follow company policy to ensure the funding is disclosed appropriately.

Travel and accommodation at sponsored meetings
Companies should pay particular attention to the planned arrangements for venues, accommodation and travel of meetings that they sponsor. It is understandable that *international* societies hold meetings in international locations. However, if a British medical

society wants to hold their meeting abroad, questions should be asked regarding why this is *necessary* from an *educational* perspective before awarding sponsorship.

Equally, travel within the UK should be carefully considered. A very good justification is needed before a Pharma company can sponsor the meeting of a Birmingham-based medical society which is to be held in Scotland. The travel arrangements should also be scrutinised to check that the travel coincides with the start and finish of the event if the company is contributing to travel costs. And if the meeting of the Birmingham-based medical society is in Birmingham, questions need to be asked if the cost includes an overnight stay! That said, when considering the need for overnight stays, it is acceptable to consider the state of regional transport networks and the impact on journey times.

Where sponsorship does include travel and accommodation costs, it is recommended that companies include relevant clauses within the sponsorship agreement so that the limit of company support is abundantly clear. Remember as well, that supporting the attendance of individuals at a meeting falls within the scope of individual disclosure, so always follow the company policy to ensure the necessary permissions are obtained.

Similar standards of hospitality should be applied to sponsored and company-organised meetings. This includes costs for accommodation and subsistence.

The extent of support provided

The extent and nature of support provided can affect the company's liability for the event and may even dictate which internal approval process should be applied to the consideration of the sponsorship involved. Some companies draw a distinction between paying a small sum for the right to erect an exhibition stand and a more generous contribution towards the overall running costs of the whole meeting. All support falls within the scope of disclosure.

Delegates at congresses

It is acceptable for companies to arrange for a group of HCPs to attend a congress as part of a structured company programme. The selection of delegates should stand up to individual scrutiny – i.e. they should be chosen for the educational benefit they would derive rather than because they are key prescribers for the company. The offer of a delegate place should not be linked to product sales in any way. All delegate support (except meals) falls within the scope of disclosure.

The arrangements for the attendance of delegates at *international* congresses should be certified by head office, as should all documentation relating to their stay (welcome packs, etc).

Exhibition stands and material

The Code places no distinction between the arrangements meetings that are organised by a healthcare organisation and ones that are organised at a private venue by a third-party company. Pharma, however may view the business justification for supporting the two types of event very differently. Note that by 'arrangements', I mean the logistics (venue, etc). There is no need for a company to review the speaker slides if it is not the company's own meeting.

From a Code perspective, it is acceptable to place an exhibition stand in the same room in which an educational meeting is taking place as long as the organiser has given their permission. However, some companies have local policies in place forbidding this.

Only approved material should be on display at the meeting. The choice of product material displayed on the stand should be carefully considered in respect of the meeting content. For example, it might be regarded as inappropriate for a company to be present at a paediatric meeting with a diabetes product licensed only for use in adults.

Everything on an exhibition stand which is attended (even in part) by a member of the sales team is typically regarded as promotional and subject to the Code. E.g. if material relating to an ongoing clinical trial is added to a stand displaying product promotion, that material becomes 'promotional' under the Code. It is not appropriate for information about ongoing clinical trials to be made available on company promotional stands unless they are within the current licence for that product and approved for that purpose. In case 2379/1/11, a company was ruled in breach of the Code for displaying on their exhibition stand a medical journal that they had sponsored. (Unfortunately, the journal included an article about the unlicensed use of their promoted product).

It is unacceptable to display product material at an event that is attended by patients or patient groups, etc. Non-promotional educational material about the medical condition may be appropriate as long as it has been certified for that purpose. MSLs should not normally be involved in events that involve patient groups or members of the public. Specific guidance should be sought from head office when such situations are likely to occur.

Company employees at independent meetings

Recent Code cases have provided additional clarity regarding the appropriate behaviour of company employees during third-party events.

Attending sessions

With agreement from the organisers, MSLs may be present in the majority of sessions at independent third-party events. However, MSLs should not be present when specific patients are discussed, for example during case review meetings.

MSLs should refrain from participating in debates or making statements about the company or its products.

"Off duty" (social) time

It is understandable that delegates may choose to explore the local area during their evenings and also that company employees might want to visit local hostelries. Great care must be taken concerning the impression created by certain activities.

A series of Code cases has now highlighted what is an acceptable level of interaction between HCPs and company employees during meetings that include evening "down time".

Historical cases had led companies to insist that it was inappropriate for employees and HCPs to be in the same social venues. Some companies even go so far as to insist that if employees enter a bar where HCPs are present, the employees must leave. This has caused some frustration amongst the employees who resented being forced to seek venues some distance from the conference centre in order to avoid HCPs when socializing with their colleagues.

However, the Appeal Board has now clarified that it is acceptable for company employees to be in the same social venue. It is the nature of the interactions that gives rise to reputational concerns for the industry, not the geographic proximity.

In other words, employees should sit at a separate table where possible; not buy drinks for the HCPs (even from their own pocket);

and should maintain a low profile. The behaviour of the employees is regarded as within the scope of the Code for the duration of their time at the conference, so late, rowdy nights are best avoided – and MSLs should not *accompany* delegates to disco-type venues (e.g. venues with music and dancing).

chapter 10

advisory boards

There are times when it is appropriate to convene a panel of advisors to provide the company with guidance on a particular subject. This is the essence of an advisory board.

On occasion, MSLs may be invited by head office to manage or to be in attendance at national or regional advisory boards. Advisory boards should always be approved by head office.

The Code's hospitality limits apply to advisory boards as they would to any other meeting. However, the critical difference between an advisory board and a promotional meeting in that the company is seeking (not giving) information. This has implications for the agenda and for the manner in which the meeting is run. It also means that it is acceptable to pay the advisors for their time since they are acting as consultants to the company.

Planning an advisory board

In order to convene an advisory board, the company must have first identified questions that it needs to answer. This is crucial – an advisory board should not be convened on a whim; if there are no questions, there is no justification for gathering the advisors.

An advisory board must therefore have clear objectives. These might be medical or scientific or for the development of marketing strategy or tactics. They can be to obtain opinion on future promotional campaigns and they can be to seek advice about the best way to position forthcoming data.

Since advisory boards are convened for the purposes of seeking advice, agendas where the 'advisors' seem to spend all their time listening are unlikely to be compliant – it is expected that a significant proportion of the agenda be dedicated to discussion. In fact, where possible, delegates should be sent pre-reading material to maximise the discussion time available at the advisory board itself. The justification for the selection of each delegate should be included in the approvals folder that is reviewed by the signatories.

Simply put, it would be wrong to choose individuals for participation in an advisory board simply because they were on a development list. The objectives of the advisory board should be determined and a short-list developed of individuals who might be able to provide the company with the necessary advice. Ranking the individuals to be invited would be acceptable – as long as it was their expertise that determined the ranking.

Also, under no circumstances whatsoever should the company or agency include objectives relating to 'advocacy development' or 'sharing information'. While this may again sound obvious, the purpose of an advisory board is to gain advice. Given that companies are paying HCPs to attend, such promotional objectives would be a very serious breach indeed.

The payment of advisors

The attendees at advisory boards are consultants or 'service providers', so they can be paid for their work. This means the advisors need to sign a written contract in a similar manner as if they were speaking at a company-organised meeting.

Honoraria must be commensurate with the time and effort involved and the professional status of the recipients, i.e. each delegate must be paid according to 'fair market value'. The level of remuneration must be appropriate to the activity being performed and the seniority of the individual. Organisers should consult the company's fair market value tables where these exist. A useful case that considers the structure of advisory boards is 2747/1/15.

At present, it is still not clear under the Code whether the reimbursement of expenses (without actual payment for services) would require a formal contract. However, since the principle of the Code's requirement for contracting is one of transparency, a company is likely to face some questions if it makes any payments to HCPs without a contract being in place – including for expenses.

By their very nature, advisory boards are convened to answer specific questions, and since the contract should usually state the specific nature of the services to be provided by the advisor, it is likely that the contract will be specific to the advisory board. In other words, it is difficult to see how a company could devise an annual contract with their 'usual' KOLs to provide 'general services' and include advisory boards on that list.

Selection of advisors

The number of participants at a meeting should be limited so as to allow active participation by all. Six to eight advisors is a more practical number than ten to twelve.

Inviting large numbers of advisors is difficult to justify since, by their nature, advisory boards are about the quality and depth of information, not about obtaining quantitative information.

Approval of advisory boards

All the content that is presented to the advisors needs to be examined by signatories (in most companies, content is actually certified via a materials approval system). The objectives, agenda, venue, costs and attendees must be carefully considered. All delegates must be chosen for their expertise, contracted for their services and paid fair market value. The rationale and honoraria amounts should all be documented and archived with the approvals folder.

Other considerations

Advisory boards should usually be attended by a member of the head office medical team.

The delegates are subject to the same hospitality limits as those that apply to promotional meetings organised by the company. This includes consideration of the suitability of the venue, subsistence limits and travel arrangements (see chapter 8 for more information).

The outputs of the advisory board must be evaluated after the event and the file annotated accordingly prior to archive. All details of the advisory board, including copies of the HCP contracts, must be formally archived and retained for at least three years.

It is important that the advisory board is clearly separated from promotional activities. There have been a number of recent cases where the association between a promotional activity and an advisory board has been deemed to be too close.

In case 2205/2/09, the delegates at an advisory board wrote a series of case studies which the company then inappropriately published as an independently produced journal supplement. In case 2290/12/09, the company concerned distributed a record of comments made by each individual advisor to members of their field-based teams; this turned the entire advisory board into a promotional activity and rendered the advisors' honoraria payments in breach of the Code as well.

Liaising with delegates

Invitations to participate in an advisory board meeting should state the purpose of the meeting, the expected advisory role and the amount of work to be undertaken. However, it should be remembered that the vast majority of communications between representatives and health care professionals are subject to the Code. This includes all letters and e-mails that are concerned with recruiting and briefing advisors, so it is important to consider the content of the invitation carefully.

The initial letter, which needs approval by head office, should state the purpose of the advisory board and enough brief information to enable the invitee to decide whether or not they might be willing to participate. On receipt of the initial indication, more detailed information can then be provided.

All delegates must have signed written contracts (including appropriate confidentiality clauses) prior to attending the advisory board. Under no circumstances is it appropriate for someone who has not signed a contract to participate in any way.

chapter 11

engagement of consultant services

Introduction

In order to conduct its business, a pharmaceutical company occasionally needs to call on the skills and knowledge of practicing healthcare professionals (HCPs) and associated administrative staff. Given that the HCPs are also potential customers, it is important that the interactions are conducted in a proper and transparent manner so that the nature of the relationship is clearly understood by all. The principles that apply to the engagement of services from HCPs apply equally to services received from patients, from administrators and from journalists, etc.

It should be quickly stated that the Code refers to 'consultants'. While the individuals may indeed hold the status of a consultant physician or consultant nurse, the term actually refers to all healthcare professionals and administrative staff who are paid directly to provide a service on behalf of the company.

Whilst it is important to recognise the independent status of HCPs, anyone acting on behalf of a company is subject to the conditions of the ABPI Code of Practice. All service providers must therefore be briefed on their obligations under the Code.

All HCPs who provide services to or on behalf of a company must be contracted to do so in a written agreement. This applies to all services supplied by UK HCPs, including any activities that take place overseas. Because all fee for service arrangements fall within the scope of disclosure, it is likely that company policy will require a written agreement even if the speaker only accepts expenses and not a fee.

There are some important practical considerations regarding the introduction of written agreements. Firstly, the contract must be signed before the service commences. This means, for example, that it would be inappropriate for speakers to sign the contract when they arrive at the venue to give the talk, because they will already have undertaken preparation and they will already have incurred expenses in travelling to the venue.

The first approach to a potential service provider should ideally be a personal visit. This allows the meeting organiser to brief the consultant about their obligations under the code and to explain objectives of the service. In the rare circumstances when it may be impractical to make the initial contact in writing, company signatories should be consulted about the content and tone of the letter or email.

There must always be a legitimate need for the service, which is clearly identified, documented and recorded. It is acceptable for the need to be directly related to the company's products (e.g. speaking at a meeting or training representatives). However, it is not acceptable for the service to be a reward for prescribing the company's products. Under no circumstances must the engagement be used as an inducement to prescribe, recommend, administer, supply, buy or sell any company product. This sounds obvious, but the documentation is important to prove why that particular consultant (service provider) was selected.

The selection of consultant must be directly related to the need. This means that a company should not 'retain' the services of consult- ants for 'general purposes' and will usually only engage individuals for specific activities. Individuals must be selected on the basis of their skills and knowledge, with no consideration as to whether the consult- ant is on a product 'target' list of top prescribers, etc.

The method by which a company validates the selection of a consultant is not mandated in the Code. In theory, it could be argued that there is a need to document a specific reason for each engagement. In practice, the agenda, etc, for the meeting will probably suffice as to the legitimacy of the event and therefore the legitimate need for a speaker. This is an untested area of the Code, however, and there are also implications under the various international laws regarding anti-corruption practices that individual companies may take into account when designing their policies.

In some companies, the line manager will be required to

authorise the selection of the consultant; in others, it may be necessary to secure medical or director-level approval. The number of service providers must be appropriate to the identified need. This means, for example, that if a chairman is not necessary for a meeting, one should not be appointed. It also means that the number of individuals at advisory boards and participating in market research, etc, should be carefully considered.

To support the justification for the selection of consultants and the number engaged, it is appropriate to retain complete records for all aspects of the service, including the need for the service; the selection of each individual; the fees involved, and copies of the signed contracts. Each company has its own template contract for standard services, such as speaker meetings. Typically, the specific details of the event and the fee involved are entered at a local level, with copies of the completed and signed agreement then stored by the legal or marketing department.

All fees paid to the speaker must be at 'fair market value' (FMV). FMV is not defined in any way at all by the Code, but the underlying principle is that two individuals of similar status providing a similar service should receive a similar fee. (So that there can be no accusations that any variation in the fee is as a result of the individual's use of company products, for example.)

Each company applies its own version of FMV tables.

There are some additional general points that companies should consider. For example, if the consultant requests that their fee is made to a healthcare organisation, then this is acceptable so long as the arrangements are clearly specified in the contract. In some circumstances it might be more appropriate if the contract was between the consultant's employer and the pharmaceutical company – for example, if a professor wants their fee paid into the department's education fund, the contract for the provision of services might be between the company and the hospital (not the individual).

If the consultant provides the service whilst they are conducting their normal NHS role (e.g. allowing a trainee to shadow them), then that contract ought to be between the company and the hospital, and the consultant should not receive payment personally unless that is specified in the contract agreed with the hospital.

Consultants providing services to a company are subject to the same hospitality limits as all other HCPs, with the exception of air travel. Where a consultant is flying overseas to conduct a service on behalf of a company, it may be appropriate that business class travel is used. However, this only applies if the sole purpose for the visit is to provide the service. If, for example, the consultant is attending an advisory board whilst at an overseas congress, then the primary purpose of the visit is the congress attendance and it would be inappropriate for the company to provide business class travel.

Disclosure & declarations

Both the company and the consultant have the obligation to make the certain aspects of the arrangements public.

Consultant declarations

All contracts specify the obligation of consultants to make appropriate declarations of interest as a result of being contracted by a pharmaceutical company. Contracts requires consultants to inform their employer of the service and should also declare the service when speaking at other related events, when writing articles, when developing guidelines or when involved in decisions about company (or competitor) products, etc.

Company Declarations (disclosure)

From 2015 onwards, companies must publish a list of named HCPs that are paid to provide services to the company. The details is provided in the chapter on disclosure. However, before companies can list the name of an individual HCP, the HCP needs to give their permission for disclosure to occur (owing to data privacy laws). Companies are approaching disclosure in different ways; some companies have elected to stop paying for services; others have detailed procedures for obtaining and recording the permissions necessary before disclosure can occur.

section 3
interactions

visits to answer medical enquiries

A key function of the MSL is to answer complex questions about company products submitted by healthcare professionals. This chapter summarises the key principles to follow.

Confirming the visit

Companies have an obligation to make information about products available to HCPs on request. This ensures that the HCP has the correct information to hand when deciding which medicine is most appropriate. However, many of the more complex questions involve discussions related to the unlicensed use of the medicine. Such questions are inappropriate for the representatives to answer and they are often passed to the MSL.

In this capacity the MSL role is akin to that of the company's medical information team and therefore enquiries should be treated in the same manner. This means logging the exact enquiry and preparing an answer that is limited to the question that has been asked.

Before visiting the customer, the MSL should confirm the question is genuine and that is has been captured correctly by the representative.

Content of medical answers

The material used by the MSL during a call to answer a medical query should be limited to the information needed to answer the question. If the HCP asks more questions, then it is acceptable to answer those questions as well, however it is not appropriate to provide information that is beyond the scope of the enquiry.

Because the MSL is answering a legitimate question, it is acceptable to provide information related to the unlicensed use of the medicine where that is appropriate.

Typically, the MSL is provided with a pre-approved slide deck that can be tailored to answer a variety of questions. If the MSL self-generates material, this should be in accordance with the company's standard SOPs for the generation of answers to medical information enquiries.

Suitability of material

It is important that material is tailored for the audience. This is because the Code requires that all material is suitable for the recipient. So, material for a diabetes specialist nurse might be different from that approved for a practice nurse in primary care. It also means that material intended for administrative staff (such as business managers) is likely to be different from that shared with HCPs.

Remember also that the definition of a 'health professional' under the Code is anyone who might prescribe, supply or administer a medicine. Everyone else who might need to know about a medicine is probably regarded as 'Other Relevant Decision Makers (ORDMs)'. In this regard, practice managers are considered ORDMs, not HCPs, so standard information material may not be appropriate for them. All material should therefore only be used for specific audiences as advised by head office.

Mailing lists

It is rarely acceptable to post or distribute material containing product information, except in response to a specific request. However, anytime the company sends anything to a customer it means that there is some form of mailing list some-where. It is a matter of *law* that mailing lists must be kept up-to-date. If a customer asks for their name to be removed, the company must act swiftly to comply. Requests for removal should be dealt with very promptly and certainly should be fully implemented within a few days of the request being received. This is why it is so important to document any requests you receive and forward them to head office quickly.

The company must be able to prove that every individual sent a promotional email has given explicit permission to receive promotional mailings about prescription pharmaceuticals. Such emails also have to meet other requirements, such as the inclusion of prescribing information and an 'unsubscribe' option, etc. The challenge for MSLs is that it is easy to inadvertently cross the line and turn an innocent email into a promotional one. So, if an MSL proactively emails a doctor and the email contains a product name, that email will almost certainly be considered promotional. If the doctor has not agreed to receive promotional email, that is a breach of the Code.

Non-promotional emails do not require the prior permission of the recipient as far as the Code is concerned. It has now been confirmed that if a customer sends an MSL an email, the Code allows the MSL to respond, however in that response, any references to product may still be regarded as promotional if they stray outside the strict bounds of answering a medical enquiry.

> In case 2116/4/08 The company was found in breach because the name of a GP remained on the mailing list after he had asked to be removed.

> In case 2094/1/08, a representative sent a non-promotional email to a consultant in connection with some medical samples. At the end of the email, the representative asked for the contact details of another HCP, saying that he wanted them in order to pass on information about a named product. The PMCPA ruled that the mention of the product for a promotional reason rendered the whole email promotional.

Promotional emails are also items of promotional material in their own right and so they are subject to the same requirements for obligatory information as all other material: Prescribing Information, AE reporting, etc.

In response to a request received at a meeting, a company employee sent some HCPs a link to a website providing official third-party guidance on how to use a particular product. The employee also copied and pasted text from the website into the email, including comments about off-licence product use. A letter from the local pharmaceutical advisor was also attached, detailing restrictions on the use of the product locally. The company employee copied the pharmaceutical advisor into the email to show openly that he was sharing the information requested. The email resulted in 8 breaches of the Code, including the fact that the email had not been approved by company signatories and that by being copied into the email, the pharmaceutical advisor was being sent what was now regarded as promotional information because he had not requested it.

Remote video calls

Video-calling is an acceptable way to manage 1:1 interactions with HCPs. However, it is appropriate to approach the interaction in the same manner as for a face-face visit.

Head office will ensure that the format of the slides used is compliant with the Code. The MSL should ensure that if they are visible in a video screen, the background behind them is a professional one.

Exhibition stand material

It is not acceptable to provide any form of gift, promotional aid or branding item to an HCP, directly or form an exhibition stand.

The only items that can be provided to individual HCPs are pens and specific items for use by patients – and even then there are strict rules. MSLs cannot give biscuits to secretaries or buy pens from a stationers to give to a GP practice; nor is it acceptable to source text books locally for distribution. Pens can be left in a room where a meeting is to take place so that the doctors can take notes. However, the pens must be supplied by head office and cannot be distributed freely. Pens cannot even be placed on an exhibition stand, because that is an inducement to visit the stand!

Items intended for patients can be provided if they are part of a formal patient support programme. Such items will be pre-approved by Head Office and issued with instructions.

Patient items can only be given directly to the HCP and cannot be distributed from an exhibition stand. (Although it is acceptable to *demonstrate* patient items on an exhibition stand and to have display copies).

Reprints

You should only ever give out official reprints of clinical papers once they have been issued to you by head office. It is not acceptable to copy the latest article from the relevant journal.

Official documents

It is not in any way acceptable to use copies of official documents for promotional purposes unless permission has been secured from the body concerned.

advanced budgetary notification (ABN)

Note: Advanced Budgetary Notification is typically undertaken by those in the NHSDM role, however it is an MSL task in some companies.

One of the main justifications for discussing information about products prior to their launch is that of budgetary impact. Essentially, where the forthcoming new product is expected to have an impact on the local NHS budget, it is appropriate to warn the budget managers.

This presupposes several points:

- Firstly, that there is a budget impact.
- Secondly, that the people being told about the budget impact have something to do with setting or managing the budget.
- Thirdly, that the information being communicated by the company is about the budget impact.

This list makes sense, but in practice it can be difficult to limit activities quite so clearly. Companies need to define who the budget holders are and what they need to know. They need to decide how far in advance to communicate, bearing in mind the commercial sensitivity of the pricing structure.

The Code recognizes that planning cycles have got shorter and there is now no specified time limit for conducting ABN. In theory budget planners need to know at least one full financial year prior to launch so they can plan the funds for the forthcoming product into the medicines budget. The closer to launch, the more difficult it is to justify calling on individuals to warn them about a budget impact, because there is less time for them to do anything about it.

Timing of announcements can be a difficult decision and is one of the many reasons why you should only act in accordance with head office instructions. And, of course, all material should be provided by and approved by head office. The budget holders need to know: the therapeutic area concerned; how much uptake there is likely to be (and why); and what the rough cost is.

If it is a me-too product with a broadly similar price, they probably don't really need to know it's coming. If it is going to halve or double the cost of treatment, then you have a reason to talk to them. If you don't know what the price is going to be, then it is difficult to justify calling on them!

Obviously, the NHS has its own horizon-scanning facilities that monitor the development of new classes of product and so at a national level, the overall scale of impact will already be accounted for. At this level, an indication of whether a single product cost is 10- 20% different from existing treatments is usually not going to matter much.

At a local level, the budget planning is generally more concerned with shorter horizons and smaller price variances. However, the price variance still has to *be of relevance* to the budget manager before you can justify calling on them in advance of having a licence.

If there is no pricing information that you can share with the budget holder, it is going to be very difficult for the PMCPA to understand why you need to warn customers about the budget impact of your new wonder-drug. There might not even be a budget impact.

If, however, the new product is going to radically alter the way in which services are delivered, then the budget impact extends beyond pure product price. For example, a new treatment that allows paramedics to treat myocardial infarction without the need for subsequent admission to A&E would definitely be of interest to budget managers, regardless of the specific cost of treatment.

Some companies ask customers to sign an agreement to confirm that they are in a position of budgetary management. This is useful information if ever the company receives a challenge regarding why that particular customer was approached.

However common sense should always be applied. Not every prescriber is a budget holder and vice-versa. It is really only acceptable to discuss budgets in advance of launch with those individuals who hold budgets at a meaningful management level. A PCO manager or the director of a hospital department is probably the lowest level at which these discussions have relevance. Prelicence discussions with a dispensary manager, or practice manager, or a typical hospital consultant are unlikely to be justifiable.

Companies need to define how the budget holders are and what they need to know. The PMCPA has indicated that if GPs are prescribing leads in clinical care commissioning groups (CCGs) and have responsibility for policy decisions on budgets then it might be reasonable to provide advanced notification to these individuals.

section 4

customer service

chapter 14

no inducements or bribes

It is unacceptable to bribe any individual to prescribe, dispense, supply, administer, recommend, buy or sell or consume a medicine. This starts with the obvious premise that it is unacceptable to pay an HCP to prescribe a specific medicine and covers all possible ground in between, right down to not being allowed to induce HCPs to visit an exhibition stand with the offer of a free pen.

Clause 18.1 specifically bans the offering of any inducement to HCPs or other relevant decision makers.

Patient support programme items

It is acceptable to give an HCP an item to pass on to patients enrolled in a patient support programme. However, it is not acceptable to give out the same items from an exhibition stand, or for to give them to the HCP for their personal use.

Pens & pads

It is acceptable to provide approved pens and pads to HCPs at meetings.

This is so that HCPs can make notes. However even here there are limits to the generosity of the company can offer. The pens & pads (together) must be under £6 in perceived value. Pens can only be provided in the meeting room (never on the exhibition stand). Pens that show the company name cannot be placed in delegate exhibition bags.

Examples of acceptable and unacceptable support

Offering/ support	Comments
Charitable donations	Companies can make a payment to a recognized charity whenever an HCP attends at exhibition stand. It is not acceptable to donate to a charity in order to gain access to an individual HCP.
Room hire	It is not acceptable to pay a primary care practice for the hire of their room in order to hold a meeting. It is also not acceptable to pay into a hospital department's "education fund" for room hire for a meeting, etc. It is acceptable to pay the hospital for room hire if that is hospital policy.
Package deals	Material & items associated with a package deal are not inducements (see chapter 14 above for more details).
Loans	Long term or permanent loans of equipment are regarded as gifts ant therefore not allowed.
Competitions & quizzes	Quizzes and competitions cannot be used for promotion. Prizes cannot be offered for quizzes, etc. Exhibition stands cannot be included in any way in a quiz.
	It is acceptable to validate learning as a pre-planned element of an educational meeting. It is not acceptable to run or sponsor a competition where individual patients win prizes. It is acceptable to run or sponsor competitions about general health where the prizes are for a healthcare organization.

DVDs & memory sticks	It is acceptable to provide educational literature on DVDs & memory sticks, since it is the content that is of value.
Literature for patients	There is no limit on literature about medicines provided via an HCP to patients. Even "story books" for children are acceptable in this Books can be supplied to healthcare organisations as MEGS (see chapter 18), but not to individual healthcare professionals.

chapter 15

providing financial support to individual HCPs

Donations and grants for the benefit of individuals

It is not acceptable make a donation or grant for the personal benefit of an individual.

However, companies can provide support to enable an HCP to attend an educational meeting or training course in order to improve the care offered to patients.

Note that some companies will only consider applications received on *behalf* of individuals or single-handed GPs from NHS management institutions, and not from individuals themselves. This gives a level of assurance that the institution is aware of, and supports, the application. It also removes any suspicion about the motivations of the company in giving money directly to named individuals. Single-handed GPs, for example, are not eligible for support in many companies.

Regardless of who makes the *application,* most companies now refuse to pay money into the bank accounts of individuals and insist on making any payments to institutional accounts.

Examples of applications that could be considered for financial support:

- Registration fees at an international congress
- Travel costs for attendance at an international congress
- Management skills/presentation skills course
- Course to improve clinical skills

Examples of applications that might not normally be approved for grants:

- Locum fees to provide cover while the applicant attends a training course
- MBAs, marketing qualifications
- Courses where the primary purpose is to gain clinical qualifications

The company may consider limiting the number of times any individual HCP can receive sponsorship.

Since 2015, there has been a requirement for pharmaceutical companies to disclose the support provided to named individual HCPs on a disclosure website established by the ABPI website. See Chapter 23 on transparency reporting for more information.

providing financial support to organisations

Providing financial support to healthcare organisations

One of the fantastic things that pharmaceutical companies do is to provide a significant level of funding to enable patient care to be enhanced, either directly or through educational opportunities for health professionals. In other words, Pharma contributes a lot of money in the form of grants and sponsorships.

Broadly speaking, there are three types of support that pharmaceutical companies are asked to give to their customers:

- Financial support to enable meetings to happen (covered in chapter 8 (meetings sponsorship))
- Support for individuals to *attend* meetings (covered in chapter 15 (individual sponsorship/ travel grants))
- Grants to organisations (covered here)

Some companies differentiate between grants (which are made to healthcare organisations), travel grants (which are made to individuals) and donations (which are made to charities). Some companies also differentiate between "restricted" and "unrestricted" grants. However, the terminology used in different companies varies considerably; as with everything in the Code, it is best to focus on what the activity is, rather than what it is called.

The Code requires that assistance can only be provided for meetings that are of educational value (from a medical perspective). The Code also requires that assistance given under Clause 19 (MEGS) is to benefit patient care, or to help the NHS as long as it does not harm patient care. The support might be in the form of financial help or other benefits in kind. However, it might also be in the form of services or goods that the company provides. This is why the Code describes the content of Clause 19 as *Medical and Educational Goods and Services (MEGS)*.

The actual terms and processes in the Code may be different from those used in any specific company– so it is important that readers absorb the *principles* and then apply the local terminology where necessary. The principles matter more than the definitions.

It is permissible for the company to make grants (including benefits in kind) to institutions, organisations or associations that are comprised of healthcare professionals and to organisations that provide healthcare or conduct research.

Such support is allowed if:

- It is made for the purpose of supporting healthcare or research
- It is documented and kept on record by the company
- It does not constitute an inducement to recommend, prescribe, purchase, supply, sell or administer specific medicinal products

It is also acceptable to make a general grant to support the administration costs for an organisation.

Donations and grants provided to organisations and institutions fall within clause 19. This means they are also classed as medical and educational goods and services so all the rules discussed in Chapter 18 apply here as well. However financial support requires additional considerations owing to the fact that money (almost literally) changes hands.

In summary:

- Financial support can only be provided to an organisation, not to an individual (apart from educational registration – see chapter 15)
- The support must be provided in the interests of patient care, the NHS (without harming patient care) or for research
- The support does not have to be strictly financial – it might be a benefit in kind (e.g. printing leaflets using company machines instead of providing money for a printer)

- There must be a written agreement between the receiving organisation and the company
- The support cannot be a *quid pro quo* for looking favourably on company products
- The nature of the company's involvement must always be transparently declared
- Both parties have to declare the support

Note that, in general, anything connected with the presence of the company at a meeting are not MEGS; and can be regarded as *meeting sponsorship*. This includes the purchase of space for an exhibition stand, declarations that the company is a "Gold sponsor" and the display of the company logo in the coffee area.

General principles

There are some general principles that apply to MEGS:

- It is unacceptable to target support on the basis of product use or for the support to be offered as any kind of inducement whatsoever.
- The decision to provide funding must be separated from the sales team (and ideally from the marketing team as well). The decision should be taken on non-commercial grounds and the onus should be on the applicant to demonstrate why the funding is required.
- Support does not have to be monetary and could include anything that could be considered to have a benefit to the recipient. The type of support could include the secondment of company employees, use of company resources, training, books and computer equipment, as well as financial contributions.
- A company can limit support according to budget availability.
- Representatives should not deliver cheques or remittance notes.
- Support is provided on the understanding that it is public and transparent. The decision to apply for funding should be supported by the applicant's senior managers.
- The company's involvement must be clear and transparent.
- The support will be disclosed on the ABPI Disclosure website.

There are some very clear principles that apply to any form of financial support, whether it is provided to individuals or organisations. The first is that the company must provide the money in order to further the interests of patient care or the NHS or research (the funding cannot be linked to commercial gain for the product). The second is that the company has an obligation to check that the money is going to be used appropriately. Finally, both the company and the recipient have to declare that support has been provided.

Leveraging a MEGS to gain a product-related advantage is regarded as completely inappropriate. In case 2984/10/17, a company was ruled in breach of the Code for providing funding that was knowingly utilised to develop a treatment protocol that was deliberately implemented to increase use of its products; the company was required to undergo an audit of its processes.

Documentation

There are two sets of required documentation. First, the provision of sufficient evidence so that the company can be sure the application is genuine and that the amount of money is appropriate. Second, a written agreement or contract, specifying the terms of the arrangement. The pharmaceutical company has an obligation to confirm that the project planned by the applicant organisation meets the requirements of the Code. Therefore, it is appropriate to ask for supporting evidence.

Usually, there should be a letter from a suitably senior manager of the applicant organisation which explains the nature of the project and how it will benefit patient care, help the NHS or support research. The letter should explain why the financial support is needed.

It is not appropriate for the sales representative to endorse the application in any way as this could be perceived as adding a sales-related motivation to the grant consideration.

If the application is successful there needs to be a written agreement between the company and the applicant. Most companies require the applicant to sign a form of contract before releasing the money. This is a good idea, however it is not a specified requirement of the code *per se*. The written agreement must specify certain conditions of funding, however. This includes why the money was provided, how much money is provided and the fact that the company does not expect any favours in return for providing it. The contract must also specify declarations and disclosures that are required by each party.

Declarations

Since 2015, every company has had to publish a list of healthcare organisations that have received grants or support as benefits in kind on the ABPI disclosure website. Companies can consider asking the *recipients* to publicly declare receipt of the funding but there is no absolute requirement for this to take place.

All material or activities that are supported by a company must carry prominent declarations of that support, which must clearly identify the nature of the support provided. This typically means on the front cover of printed material and on every relevant page of websites. The need for a declaration applies to all related documents issued by the funding recipient. E.g. if the company funds the printing costs of a booklet, then the booklet itself and any material advertising the existence of the booklet must all carry a declaration of Pharma funding. Where the company has supported staff posts, the individuals in those posts must be aware that the company has contributed some or all of their salary.

Representative Involvement

While not specifically stated in the Code itself, case rulings have demonstrated a negative perception whenever sales representatives are involved in the provision of grants; no such issues have yet been raised in relation to MSLs, however the external perception must always be borne in mind. Decisions about who gets support should typically be made by representatives.

However, there is nothing wrong in MSLs helping the customer understand *how* to apply to the company for funding so long as it is clear that the MSLs has no influence over the decision.

Types of project

There are certain activities and materials that companies should normally avoid supporting:

- Competition prizes
- Locum costs
- Departmental newsletters
- Blogs or on-line chat rooms

Type of applicant

Companies have become concerned about the provision of grants to general practice. This is for several reasons, but mainly connected with the GP contract and the way in which GPs are paid. Essentially, by undertaking certain activities, practice incomes increase. GPs are partners in the practice and therefore their personal incomes increase as a result of the additional activities. The suspicion therefore arises that the motivation for the project is one of personal gain rather than enhanced patient care.

Some companies have decided to only accept funding applications from general practice if they are received from the senior partner or the practice manager. However, the company may also consider seeking endorsement from a higher management institution if it has any doubts about providing the support. For example, where a practice is seeking money for a pilot project, which would lead to it subsequently seeking ongoing funding from the Primary Care Organisation (PCO), it may be appropriate to ensure that the PCO supports the need for the improved patient care that the project will potentially deliver. The ongoing changes in the structure of the NHS within primary care are likely to add to the complexity here.

Targeting of support

Since donations must be unconnected with product sales, it is very difficult to justify targeting them in a particular geographic area – and even more difficult to justify targeting them in a specific general practice or hospital.

Return on investment (ROI)

Given that companies should make grants in a way that is unconnected with their products, it is not acceptable to calculate the ROI.
This is because the reason the donations are made is to enhance the
reputation of the company.

Contracts typically include

- Purpose of the project
- Amount involved
- Details of payment process
- Any non-financial support provided by the company
- A statement that support provided by the company is unconnected with
  use of company products by the applicant
- A statement that the pharma company will declare the details of the
  funding publicly
- A requirement for documents about the project to include statements of
  sponsorship by the company
- A request for/permission for the recipient to publicly declare receipt of
  funding at any other time (e.g. on recipient's website)
- Data protection statements – permission to retain applicant's details on
  file, for example
- Start and end dates to the funding
- Statements absolving the company of any further liability for the project
  beyond the provision of funding
- References to the Code (e.g. venue selection)

Note that individual companies may incorporate some or all of the
types of support listed in this section within various internal policies.

chapter 17

providing non-financial support to healthcare organisations (MEGS, etc)

The pharmaceutical industry has a proud tradition of providing services that improve patient care and support the NHS. The clause in the Code that affects the provision of Medical and Educational Goods and Services (MEGS) is clause 19. This clearly states that the MEGS must enhance patient care; or benefit the NHS and maintain patient care.

There is a wide range of possible support that falls within the scope of MEGS. This includes books, training programmes, equipment, finance and therapeutic reviews. Where the company *proactively* offers an actual service or item, this falls within the scope of clause 19.1, which we consider here. Where the company provides support in the form of finance (usually having received a *request* for support), this should usually be considered first as a grant under clause 19.2 (see chapter 17).

The provision of MEGS is strictly non-promotional and should not be connected with the sales of any individual products. For example, it is unacceptable to target support on the basis of product use, or for the provision of MEGS to be offered as any kind of inducement. Nor is it acceptable to limit availability of MEGS to a 'target' doctors or target practices or only to practices that prescribe company products.

In fact, the manner in which the clause is enforced by the PMCPA makes it clear that companies and their employees must make *every* effort to avoid even implying a link between MEGS and their products.

Approval and documentation

Just about everything connected with the provision of MEGS should be reviewed and certified by company signatories. This includes: briefing material for representatives; all customer-facing and patient-facing material and communications; the service protocol, and all operational documents pertaining to the service.

For all MEGS, the recipient must be given a written protocol. In most companies this means establishing a written agreement between the recipient and the company. Regardless of the format the document takes, it needs to contain certain key points of clarification for all concerned and needs to be certified.

The contract should specify:

* The role and identity of the pharmaceutical company.
* The recipients' understanding of all the arrangements, including any reports they will receive, any data that the pharmaceutical company will collect and what the company will do with the data.

It is also helpful if the contract clearly states the absence of any implied commitment from the practice to the Pharma company

Under no circumstances should any application for MEGS be supported with a 'business justification'. Provision must be based on the needs of the recipient and must be unconnected with the company's local sales interests.

Transparency

The MEGS must be clearly identified as having been provided or sponsored by a pharmaceutical company. This means an appropriate statement on all materials and during all discussion. For example, the service provider should clearly identify themselves to HCPs and patients as having been financed by the pharmaceutical company concerned.

Disclosure

Since 2015, companies have been required to declare the value of any medical services provided to healthcare organisations on the ABPI's disclosure website.

chapter 18

joint working with healthcare organisations

Joint Working is defined by the PMCPA and the Department of Health as: "situations where, for the benefit of patients, one or more pharmaceutical companies and the NHS pool skills, experience and/or resources for the joint development and implementation of patient centred projects and share a commitment to successful delivery".

Joint Working is still a developing area in practical implementation as well as with respect to case law. The Department of Health and the ABPI published a joint toolkit in 2008, and this contains some excellent project management tools, but very little governance information and went largely unnoticed by the NHS itself. The ABPI has published guidance that is referred to in the Code, however the Code makes the point that the ABPI guidance goes further than the Code requires (although it then goes on to say that companies should take the ABPI and DoH documents into account . . .).

What is Joint Working?

Joint Working is a partnership between the NHS and Pharma (and sometimes with other parties). It is where the NHS and Pharma share a common goal and which they pool resources to achieve. However, it is important to realise that it is a partnership – each party must make a 'significant contribution'.

The ABPI guidance defines a 'significant' contribution as each contributing to projects exceeding £15,000 in value, however the Code is silent on what 'significant' means. The ABPI guidance also implied that Joint Working projects should usually last more than 6 months; again the Code is silent on this point.

Joint Working publications

ABPI Guidance Notes On Joint Working Between Pharmaceutical Companies And The NHS And Others For The Benefit Of Patients Taking Into Consideration The 2008 ABPI Code Of Practice For The Pharmaceutical Industry (published by the ABPI in 2009)

NHS Best Practice Guidance on joint working between the NHS and the pharmaceutical industry and other relevant commercial organisations. A toolkit, Moving Beyond Sponsorship: joint working between the NHS and the pharmaceutical industry (published by the Department of Health & the ABPI in 2008)

There is also brief Guidance issued in 2012, however this is so brief it can actually be misleading from a Code perspective

The scope of what constitutes a Joint Working project is limited by the imagination of the partners – with one key consideration. The project must have a defined patient outcome benefit.

The difference between Joint Working and MEGS

Apart from the fact that both parties contribute to the project, the differences between Joint Working and MEGS activities are significant. The main consideration is that while Joint Working must be for the benefit of patients, it is *expected* that the arrangements will also benefit the pharmaceutical company!

This means that the company can target Joint Working activities in areas where it will benefit commercially. In fact, Joint Working can even be based on the use of a particular medicine by a healthcare organisation. The only real stipulation is that the parties must have satisfied themselves that the use of the medicine will enhance patient care and that treatments must be in line with nationally accepted clinical guidance where such exists. There is, of course, a strong argument that *all* medicines enhance patient care because the products are licensed for that reason by the MHRA. In effect this means that Pharma can co-fund projects that implement NICE guidance, and national society guidelines – and where guidelines do not exist Pharma can co-fund any project that uses medicines to enhance patient care. Common sense would suggest that the Pharma company's product should already be on formulary so that the use of a particular medicine is not a condition of funding – and this is what the ABPI guidance specifies. However, there is no such requirement in the Code itself.

That said, a *quid pro quo* for a formulary listing is not appropriate. Rather, the consideration should be that is acceptable to choose projects that will grow the local market for the relevant disease area. So, for example, a company can choose to support a project in an area where they are already on the formulary (and will therefore gain additional sales as a result). Equally, they can reject projects in areas where they are not on the formulary. However, it is not ok to demand product placement in return for support.

It is also not acceptable for any individual or individual practice to benefit directly from Joint Working – the NHS benefits must be accrued by hospitals and NHS management organisations.

It is also acceptable to partner directly with the private sector and to contract with the private sector to deliver the Joint Working project.

Governance & declarations

Everything must be conducted in an "open and transparent manner". This means that an executive of all Joint Working projects must be declared on the company website at the *outset* of the project. There is no absolute requirement for the NHS to publish an executive summary, although it is 'encouraged' to do so.

In addition, all financial investment by pharmaceutical companies in relation to Joint Working must be disclosed regardless of whether the partner or a third party receives the money.

The outcome of all projects must be measured, usually monitoring progress against a set of baselines. It would be helpful if the outcomes were also published as part of the concluding executive summary, although the Code does not mandate this.

All outputs from Joint Working projects should be labelled with a statement indicating the nature of the pharmaceutical company's involvement (in order to comply with clause 9.10).

The company is required to certify all outputs from Joint Working, except the agreement itself. The one case that involves certification of Joint Working projects clarified in crystal clear fashion that the Appeal Board and PMCPA will not accept any excuses in this regard and that failing to certify is regarded as bringing the industry into disrepute.

Interactions

The ABPI guidance requires that discussions and agreements should take place at a senior level within the NHS and the pharmaceutical company, such as "authorised negotiators" or "signatories" of the Trust and Directors within the Pharma company. However, there is no requirement within the Code itself for this.

The expectations for Joint Working projects are that they will not usually be between Pharma and GP Practices or hospital departments. It is understood that the practical implementation might take place at a local or departmental level, however the agreement must be at a high level within the local NHS management structure.

The written agreement must include:

- name of the joint working project
- parties to the agreement, specifying all aspects of input
- date and term of the agreement
- expected benefits for patients, the NHS and the pharmaceutical company; patient benefits should always be stated first
- how patient benefits and the success of the project will be measured, when and by whom
- an outline of the financial arrangements
- roles and responsibilities of the NHS and the pharmaceutical company
- the planned publication of any data or outcomes
- if a pharmaceutical company enters into a joint working agreement on the basis that its product is already included in an appropriate place on the local formulary, a clear reference to this should be included in the joint working agreement so that all the parties are clear as to what has been agreed
- contingency arrangements to cover possible unforeseen circumstances such as changes to summaries of product characteristics and updated clinical guidance
- a dispute resolution clause

- disengagement/exit criteria including an acknowledgement by the parties that the project might need to be amended or stopped if a breach of the Code is ruled
- the requirement that the pharmaceutical company must publish an executive summary of the joint working agreement and disclose the money it invests; the NHS organisation should also be encouraged to publish the arrangements

information for patients

It is acceptable for companies to answer questions posed by patients – however these must be answered through medical information teams. MSLs should never interact directly with patients or patient organisations without explicit instruction from head office.

It is important to recognise that patient organisations are comprised of members of the general public. It is not appropriate to discuss medicines with them, or to present product information at patient organisation meetings.

The Code requires that all information provided to patients about medicines and diseases requires certification. It is also important to remember that all information provided to patients must include the relevant adverse event reporting statement.

Patient Support Programmes

A growing area of patient communications is the provision of Patient Support Programmes (PSPs). Such programmes are typically designed to improve adherence to treatment by assisting patients in better understanding their medical condition and the treatment they are receiving. The concept is simple. Pharmaceutical companies provide a package of support to help patients understand their illness, their medicine and how to make lifestyle changes to improve the treatment of their condition. This might include teaching patients how to administer an injection properly, reminders to take tablets, information about a disease and dietary advice. It might involve patients having access to telephone-based support services from qualified nurses or being given access to specific websites.

As part of a PSP, it is acceptable for companies to provide patients with items that would help them comply with treatment. These items can only be supplied when they are part of a formal patient support programme; they cannot be supplied as standalone items. These items are defined in Clause 18.2. Any items provided as part of a PSP must be directly related to the treatment of the relevant illness.

disclosure of transfers of value

Public scrutiny of industry activities has led to increasing willingness by the industry to be transparent regarding its financial interactions with customers and other stakeholders. As a result, the Code includes some specific requirements regarding the transparency of company expenditure with regards to meetings, honoraria and associated expenses and enhanced reporting for interactions with patient organisations.

Since 2015, pharmaceutical companies have published the details of all transfers of value to individual HCPs and HCOs on the ABPI Disclosure website.

Support provided to patient groups continue to be announced on the websites of the individual companies.

Patient Organisations

Supported projects (money or benefits in kind)

The information related to the preceding calendar year must be published by 1st July on the company website. The declarations must an indication of value of benefits in kind.

Companies must declare:

- Name of Patient Group
- Project supported
- Amount donated / value of benefits received

Commissioned services

The information related to the preceding calendar year must be published by 1st July on the company website. The declarations must an indication of value of benefits in kind.

Companies must declare:

- Nature of service provided
- Amount paid in fees
- Amount paid in expenses

Healthcare Organisations

Supported projects (money or benefits in kind)

The information related to the preceding calendar year must be published by 1st July on the ABPI Disclosure website.

Companies must publish:

- Name of organisation
- Project supported
- Amount donated / value of benefits received

There includes support provided as Medical & Educational Goods and Services.

Joint Working Projects

Companies must continue to publish an executive summary of all Joint Working projects, including the financial arrangements, at the commencement of the project on the company website. However, these are also regarded as "Transfers of Value" to the organization under the Code and so the value will be published on the ABPI Disclosure website as well.

Commissioned services

Where companies commission services from HCOs, the information related to the preceding calendar year must be published by 1st July on the ABPI Disclosure website.

Companies must publish:

* Nature of service provided
* Amount paid in fees
* Amount paid in expenses

Individual HCPs

Support to attend meetings (money or benefits in kind)
The information related to the preceding calendar year must be published by 1st July on the ABPI Disclosure website.

Companies must declare:

* Name of HCP
* Amount of sponsorship provided for:
  ○ *Registration fees (UK or overseas)*
  ○ *Travel (UK or overseas)*
  ○ *Accommodation (UK or overseas)*

Commissioned services
The information related to the preceding calendar year must be published by 1st July on the ABPI Disclosure website.

Companies must declare:

* Name of HCP
* Nature of service provided
* Amount paid in fees
* Amount paid in accommodation expenses (UK or overseas)
* Amount paid on travel expenses (UK or overseas)

Permission to disclose

Where the HCP does not give permission to disclose the transfers of value against their name, the company must still disclose the sums involved. In this case, they will disclose a total amount that encompasses all the transfers where permissions were not obtained.

HCOs cannot opt out of disclosure, only individuals.

sponsor

compliancehub
creative compliance solutions

Our aim is to help clients comply with the various codes and regulations that impact the marketing of medicines and medical devices. We aim to deliver creative compliance solutions and the best possible customer experience.

Our services encompass: Consultancy, Audit and Training, however within these general headings is a deceptively broad range of client-focused support. Our public workshops are designed to support signatories, review teams and compliance officers in their personal development.

We offer bespoke solutions to high quality customer service and the delivery of practical and creative compliance solutions to high quality customer service and, the delivery of practical and creative compliance solutions.

Our services include:

- Signatory Training – Compliance hub runs personalised in-house signatory training courses for several UK and international companies. Our public courses are exceptionally popular owing to the opportunities for interactions with peers in other companies. Aspiring signatories looking for a remotely-access development programme that can be completed at their own pace should consider our unique iSignatory e-coaching course
- Audit Services – Compliance Hub has a reputation for insightful, pragmatic audits. These include simple reviews of material

approval folders through to gap identification in systems and processes

- Consultancy Services – We have experience in a wide range of consultancy projects. Standard services include interim compliance officers, remote signatory services, complaint management and SOP development
- E-learning – We have developed custom content for numerous clients both in the UK and internationally. Compliance Hub e- 134
- Books – *The Code Explained* is a user-friendly guide to the implementation of the Code, full of practical tips and case examples. *The Pharma Rep's Code Explained* collates those aspects of the code that are most relevant to field-based sales teams into a pocket-sized quick reference book.

For more information on any of these services or resources, please contact:

Compliance Hub Unit 4, Water End Barns, Eversholt, MK17 9EA
01525 292020
www.compliance-hub.com
enquiries@compliance-hub.com

Index